CAMPING IN THE SAHARA

by

E. M. HULL

ILLUSTRATED WITH PHOTOGRAPHS
TAKEN BY *C. W. HULL*

NEW YORK
DODD, MEAD AND COMPANY
1927

Printed in Great Britain

CONTENTS

CHAP.		PAGE
I	TOUGGOURT AND TAMELHAT	9
II.	HADJÏERA THE HAUNTED	30
III.	THE MOZABITES	53
IV.	STORMBOUND	77
V.	BANDITS	99
VI.	THE GARDEN IN THE WILDERNESS	123
VII.	NOMADS	144
VIII.	OUARGLA AND A NIGHT MARCH	167

LIST OF ILLUSTRATIONS

Facing page

A STREET IN TOUGGOURT 12

THE MARKET-PLACE IN TOUGGOURT 14

A STREET IN TAMELHAT 16

THE *PLONGEURS* 20

THE LATE MESSAOUD BEN AKLI AND SIDI LAÏD TIDJANI (ON RIGHT) 24

THE DESERTED TOWN (HADJÏERA) 32

MOHAMMED SEGHIR BEN SMAIL, CAID OF HADJÏERA . 36

THE HAUNTED MARKET-PLACE, HADJÏERA . . . 38

THE CAID'S PALACE 44

THE CAID AND HIS LITTLE NIECE 46

THE CAID AND HIS ENTOURAGE 50

OUR CAMP OUTSIDE GUERRARA 60

THE WALLED CITY OF GUERRARA 62

THE MARKET-PLACE AT GUERRARA 64

MOZABITES AT GUERRARA 66

GHARDAIA AT FLOOD-TIME 68

THE DRY BED OF THE OUED N'SA 78

OUR CAMP IN THE RAVIN DU SALUT 84

A WELL IN THE DESERT 94

OUR CARAVAN ON THE MARCH THROUGH THE BANDIT COUNTRY 104

METLILI, THE BANDIT STRONGHOLD 108

" THE MAN OF FORTY-FIVE MURDERS " . . . 118

LIST OF ILLUSTRATIONS

Facing page

THE APPROACH TO EL-GOLÉA 126

THE MOSQUE AT EL-GOLÉA 132

THE GARDENS OF EL-GOLÉA 136

ONE OF OUR CAMPS IN THE NOMAD COUNTRY . . 150

NOMADS ROUNDING UP SHEEP TO MILK . . . 162

THE HEAVENLY TWINS 167

A STREET IN OUARGLA 172

THE MARKET-PLACE IN OUARGLA 176

OUR STAFF 178

A CONCERT IN THE COOK TENT 182

CAMPING IN THE SAHARA

I

TOUGGOURT AND TAMELHAT

IT was two years since our last visit to Touggourt.

Warned in the meantime that progress and civilization were advancing into the desert by leaps and bounds, we approached it again with misgivings. So when at last, late on a hot Sunday afternoon, the train from the north wound slowly into the tiny terminus, it was cheering to find that the town was still unaltered and unspoiled.

Nothing was new, except the fussy little Ford car that was waiting to bump and jolt us over the sandy half-mile to the hotel.

Our kit deposited, we went out into the market-place to renew acquaintance with people and places, accompanied by Si Aly Sab, a Kabyle landowner who was again kindly acting as caravan leader for the trip.

In the cool of the afternoon the square was full of animation.

Groups of Arabs of all classes, their flowing

burnouses ranging from the spotless white of the well-to-do to the drab mud colour of the beggar, drifted past in twos and threes or squatted by the open shops talking, eternally talking.

A string of camels, in charge of wild-eyed desert men and hung with heavy, pendulous sacks stuffed with henna from the south, stalked disdainfully through the crowd with a soft pad-pad of cushioned feet, on their way to the *fondouk*. Crouched in the sand and dust, ragged and filthy hawkers of sweetmeats and vegetables cursed shrilly when bare-legged boys, clad only in a single garment open to the waist, drove too close to their little stock-in-trade tiny donkeys staggering almost hidden under loads of brushwood and greenstuffs. Here and there the scarlet cloak of a Spahi, the striking black or brown of a chief's burnous, the vivid, clinging draperies of some veiled woman, made a splash of colour that arrested attention.

Closely buttoned to the throat in his khaki tunic, alien to his surroundings and probably dreaming of the Paris he so seldom saw, an occasional French officer hurried in the direction of the distant barracks, acknowledging perfunctorily as he went the salutes of grinning Soudanese privates.

More in keeping with the Eastern scene, a tall, black-bearded *maharist*, in the tight frock-coat and long, baggy trousers of the Saharan Camel Corps, stood the admired centre of an eager circle of friends, telling of his experiences in far-away Timimoun.

Dodging the swaying camels, the panicky rush of a score of bleating goats that were being driven in from pasture for the night, and the pigeons that were strutting between our feet, we passed on through the chattering, ever-moving throng of Arabs, negroes, Jews, and half-castes to a more open space in the market-place where a crowd was gathered round a half-naked dervish dancer. This particular dervish is a well-known figure in the annual religious processions. At the moment he was employing his spare time in making a little money on his own account. From him we turned to the greater interest of meeting again those who for weeks had been waiting and watching for our coming. These were members of our caravan, scouring the town for forgotten necessaries remembered at the last moment, men who had travelled with me before and whom I had learned to know and trust, all now wildly excited at the prospect of the new trip which was to take them, as well as ourselves, into fresh country and farther into the south than we had ever been before.

First it was our old cook Kharbouch who, in spotless gandoura and burnous, bore down on us with outstretched hands, salaaming and voluble and full of importance—for did not a large measure of our comfort weigh heavily on his capable shoulders?—mingling inquiries for our health with lists of groceries, and reassuring himself that it was indeed Evian water we wished to drink.

Then, appearing suddenly as if from nowhere in his own noiseless fashion, tall, lean Mohammed, our chief guide and tracker, shy and tongue-tied as we had always known him. And, with him, his aide, Lakada the flute-player, whose little bright eyes twinkled merrily when we inquired for the beloved instrument that lay tucked away in the pocket of his wide trousers.

And while we talked, one by one came camel-drivers, some of whom we knew already, others whose worth we had yet to prove. Among them was an old friend, Maama, a particularly graceful and neat-footed man whom years ago we had nicknamed "the Sentimentalist," noted for his dancing—the star turn, in fact, of the concert parties we had some nights sitting round the camp fire.

Laughing and talking all together, they swept us away to a big shed on the outskirts of the town where our stores and equipment were collected.

Here were more old friends, who crowded round to welcome us and chatter. The daylight was almost gone, and outside in the dusky street a knot of camel owners, seeking to drive an eleventh-hour bargain, argued and disputed heatedly, while their evil-tempered charges gurgled and roared a running accompaniment.

A STREET IN TOUGGOURT

The lofty shed, lit by spluttering acetylene flares, was a regular storehouse. A whole armoury of modern guns, old flint-locks, and ancient Kabyle weapons, decorated the walls, and ropes and saddles hung from crossbars in the roof. The floor space was congested; the atmosphere thick with acetylene fumes, cigarette smoke, and the hot, stuffy smell of cordage and crudely-dressed leather.

Skipping over boxes and bales, we counted cases of groceries and mineral water, poked rolled-up bundles of tents, inspected camel and mule saddles, and finally stubbed our toes on an innocent-looking sack which, soft to all outward appearance, in reality contained a large quantity of strong iron tent-pegs that would be required when we crossed the rocky Hamada, the region of high stone plateaux.

We lingered for some time, sitting on a couple of empty water drums, watching the busy scene about us. There was a good deal yet to do, for some of the men were only just back from a trip to Tozeur. But our start was promised for the next day, and we knew the men would not fail us even though they might have to work half the night to finish their preparations.

It was quite dark when at length we wandered back to the hotel, stumbling across the sombre patches between the jutting rays of light projected from the open shop doors. More darkly mysterious than ever appeared the entrance to the oldest part of Touggourt, that ancient labyrinth of underground streets and houses where one moves in total darkness, hearing but not seeing the passers-by, who come and go with a faint rustle of flowing robes and the slip-slap of heelless slippers.

With the late Messaoud ben Akli of Biskra we explored it some years ago, but I have never been able to discover its real origin, whether it was built for purposes of defence or merely as a protection against the hot sun of summer.

Returning through the market-place, I inquired for the old mad marabout who for years sat there day and night swaying in the dust, droning the Koran, or soothing his restless soul with the wild, strange melodies he drew from his little wooden flute. But Touggourt had recently entertained a French general, a rare enough occurrence to demand some special effort on the part of the authorities, and in a frenzy of cleanliness and order the poor old marabout, with other odd trifles, had been swept away from his accustomed niche—but not very far away, however. A few steps down a side street we found him huddled over a tiny fire of brushwood, a windbreak of dry palm fronds at his back, muttering to himself, while he stared with glazed eyes into the flickering firelight—incredibly dirty, incredibly old, but an object of veneration to his fellow citizens despite the French Government.

At night Touggourt is a peaceful town, and

14

I went to sleep hearing only the dry rustle of a palm tree near my window. A couple of hours later, however, I woke to the sound of a smashing crash that sent me out of bed clutching an electric torch.

But it was only a distracted American, one of a party of tourists, who had dropped his bedroom lamp on the stone floor of the corridor while searching for luggage that had gone astray, and who spent the best part of the next hour tramping heavily up and down the echoing passages, roaring for the guide and bewailing his lost clothes.

I never knew whether he found them or whether he, still clothesless, formed one of the motley crowd who stood in every stage of dress and undress on the hotel balcony to watch us ride away at seven o'clock next morning.

We were a fair-sized caravan. C. and I rode mules which had been specially brought down for our use from the Kabyle Mountains, in view of the rocky country ahead of us; with us were Si A. S., seven men and sixteen camels; and, tailing at the end of the procession, two baby camels, running with their mothers, whom we christened " the Heavenly Twins." They were a quaint pair, full of life and spirits, and though we lost Angelica a few weeks later, when her mother went sick, Diavolo remained with us for the whole trip and grew mightily before he saw Touggourt again.

CAMPING IN THE SAHARA

The first day's stage being always a short one, and our way leading us past Temacin and Tamelhat, we decided to stop at the latter village, and call on our old acquaintance Sidi Laïd Tidjani, the chief of the Tidjania Brotherhood, and one of the most important marabouts in Algeria.

It was a beautiful morning, with a light fresh wind, and the way lay clear before us.

We knew thoroughly the road to Tamelhat, so for the first few miles we set ourselves to become acquainted with our riding mules. They were big strong animals, well broken even to gun-fire, but with typically hard mouths. Both were wonderfully sure-footed, for which later on we were to be thankful, and both could climb like cats. C.'s was an even-tempered creature, of lamb-like docility, who on the march was calmly indifferent to everything except rat-holes, which in some parts of the desert pit the ground with treacherous little cavities that give way under the foot. These she would avoid with lively demonstrations of dislike that seemed to prove an earlier and painful acquaintance. My beast was of a different sort, full of tricks and given to wholly incomprehensible fits of bolting. I never discovered whether it was nerves or merely temper. But, oddly enough, my bundle of contrariness would stand like a rock to be shod, while it took eight men to hold the "lamb" when it was a question of a new set of shoes.

A STREET IN TAMELHAT

Shortly after leaving Touggourt we overtook a solitary *maharist* making his way back to some outpost in the south after three months' leave. He joined our caravan for a day or two, the first of several interesting characters who were to attach themselves to us for shorter or longer periods during the trip. His *mahari*—riding camel— was hung round like a Christmas-tree with rifle, blankets and burnous, grain bags, goat-skin water sack, and cooking-pots.

About a mile outside of Temacin we passed a well-remembered side turning, where two years before we had struck across country in search of a party of *plongeurs* who were said to be operating on a well in the next village. But accuracy is rarely an Arab attribute, and we rode through many villages, growing hotter and thirstier as we went, before at last we hunted down our quarry. I do not know the Arabic word for their calling. The French refer to them simply as *les plongeurs*, the divers. Their function is to descend to the bottom of wells that are fed by underground rivers, and clear away the accumulation of mud and fibrous matter which collects at the mouth of the inlet and chokes the steady inrush of water. It is an ancient and hereditary trade, which is fast dying out, for the building of artesian and other more modern styles of well is putting an end to the activities of the old *plongeurs*, and the younger generation are not following in the footsteps of their forefathers. I was therefore anxious to see these survivors of a medieval occupation while I had the opportunity, for, as at that time it was said that only twelve of the old craftsmen remained alive in Algeria, the chance might never come again. And since one of the men we saw at work that morning was considerably over seventy years of age, there are probably fewer now.

We had almost given up hope of finding the famous *plongeurs*, almost come to believe that their existence was but a pleasant myth with which to beguile innocent travellers, when at length we came to a village where the often-repeated question did not meet with a grave shake of the head and the intimation that, like poor Jo, we must still be " a-moving on." Instead quite half a dozen workers in the little gardens flung down their tools and gathered enthusiastically to guide us to the scene of operations—the excuse for a rest being too good to miss.

We arrived at the exact moment. A *plongeur* was just preparing to descend.

Stripped to a loin-cloth, standing already waist deep in the water on a rope ladder, the diver was bending forward with his hands gripping the edge of the well, taking deep breaths and clearing his throat and lungs of all fluid and matter, while hanging over him was the chief of the little company, muttering prayers and incantations and massaging him vigorously between the shoulders.

Then, almost before we could set our watches

to time him, the diver slipped down the ladder and the water closed over his head. It seemed hours before he reappeared. In reality it was three and a half minutes. Seven minutes is said to be the limit these men can remain immersed, though the late Messaoud ben Akli, who was with us at the time, told me that five minutes was the longest time he had ever seen. The obstructing rubbish collected from the inlet of the well is put into a skin bag which the diver carries tied round his waist.

When at last our man's head rose above water again the filled bag was taken from him, and he was caught and held by the headman, who thumped and massaged and prayed over him once more, while he gasped and coughed and spat until he had recovered sufficient breath to half clamber, half be dragged out of the well. Hastily smothered in thick coverings, he was then laid down beside a blazing brushwood fire.

The diving exhausts them, and for half an hour or so afterwards they are more or less in a state of collapse. One reason for this may be the fact that they are ordinarily very small eaters, and when actually at work fast for twelve hours before starting operations, with the result that they are incredibly thin—walking skeletons, in fact. If there is real necessity for this abstinence, or whether it is all part of the ritual of their calling, I was not able to discover.

They were a silent set of men, but seemed

pleased at our interest, and grouped themselves obligingly to be photographed.

We watched two or three more descents, but there was no improvement on the period of immersion, for they had every one been down several times that morning and were tired out.

With no *plongeurs* to-day to tempt us from the road, we jogged on quietly until a curve in the route revealed the tall brick minaret and rather untidy village of Temacin. It is a rich oasis boasting over fifty thousand palm trees, but beyond the minaret, which is of somewhat unique construction, it exhibits no feature of outstanding interest.

Another two miles brought us to the walled and fortified Zaouïa of Tamelhat. A Zaouïa, properly speaking, is a college or religious centre, and that of Tamelhat is a complete little township in itself. It is the headquarters of the Grand Marabout Sidi Laïd Tidjani, the chief of the Brotherhood of the Order of Tidjania, one of the most noted of the Mohammedan sects. The Brotherhood of the Tidjania was founded by the Sherif Sidi-el-Hadj Ali at the beginning of the thirteenth century. His tomb, surrounded by a very fine grille of hammered iron, is in the mosque at Tamelhat. The Order is distinguished, among other things, for its broad-mindedness, and rejects many of the petty restrictions still practised by other Mohammedan sects. This was demonstrated by a little incident that happened when I first visited the Zaouïa of Tamel-

THE PLONGEURS

hat some years ago. On that occasion Sidi Laïd
was waiting at the door of the mosque to show
us the tomb of the famous founder of the Brotherhood. Seeing that C. and I were preparing,
according to custom, to remove our long riding-
boots, he prevented us, saying smilingly that he
would take the will for the deed, since he knew
how difficult were our boots to put off and on. It
was very hot when we reached the walls of Tamelhat. And, riding through the massive wooden
gateway, we found the shady coolness of the
narrow streets and dim archways a pleasant contrast to the heat and glare outside.

Our decision to revisit the Zaouïa having been
made at the last moment, there had not been time
to advise the Grand Marabout of our coming, but
fortunately we found him at home.

Hardly were we dismounted when several
members of his family arrived to usher us up a
winding stone staircase and across an open gallery
to the long, sparsely-furnished reception-room.
Nothing was altered since our last visit, so we
spent the few minutes of waiting in removing sand
goggles and trying to reduce our extremely heated
appearance. Sidi Laïd came bustling in at last,
smiling and hospitable as ever, waving a pair of
field-glasses, through which he said he had been
watching our caravan from the roof of his house
for the last half-hour, wondering who we could be.

Nearly seven feet in height, and built in proportion, the Grand Marabout is one of the biggest

Arabs I have ever seen. Extremely intelligent, talking French fluently, though with a complete disregard for tenses, he is not only one of the foremost priests in his country, but is also a shrewd, level-headed man with a keen eye to business. Said to be one of the richest Arabs in the Sahara, he gives largely to charity and is noted for his wide and extensive hospitality.

He was followed almost immediately by a servant bringing the inevitable mint tea, which always seems to be on tap in every Arab household. After our dusty ride we were very grateful for the three glasses which custom decrees and etiquette obliges one to take.

This refreshing drink, which is consumed in quantities by all classes of Algerian Arabs, is made of green tea, with plenty of sugar, and flavoured with handfuls of fresh or dried mint.

We had planned to make only a short call at the Zaouïa. But Sidi Laïd insisted we should remain for lunch, reminding us that on our previous visit we had arrived during the afternoon and so had deprived him of the pleasure of offering us any real hospitality. All protests—for three unexpected guests at short notice seemed rather a tax on his kindness—and the fact that our own picnic basket was waiting down below in the courtyard, were swept away with the laughing remark that he would eat our lunch and we should eat his. So the basket was promptly ordered up, and Sidi Laïd ate our eggs and chicken while we did full justice to an enormous bowl of remarkably good cous-cous.

There was much of common interest to discuss during lunch, for our host was well up in current events, both internal and international. Also, since our last visit, we had had the pleasure of meeting his near relatives at the Zaouïa of Guémar, near El-Oued in the Souf, where he himself goes every year to stay during the hottest part of the summer, to avoid the fever which is then prevalent in the Touggourt and Temacin district.

The lunch table was set in an alcove in the room, and throughout the meal we could hear distinctly through the thin partition walls the echo of children's laughter and the sound of women's voices talking unceasingly.

Mohammedan priests are not celibate, nor usually monogamous, as are the majority of the secular chiefs in Algeria nowadays. And we realized that the voices we heard were those of his wives and other female members of his household. We should have liked an opportunity of meeting them, but Sidi Laïd did not suggest a visit to his harem, so we could only ignore the perfectly audible buzz of conversation, though we knew very well that without doubt we ourselves were the subject of discussion. And we wondered what those hidden women—by now assuredly in full possession of detailed descriptions of ourselves, our features, and our clothing—were saying and thinking of the Englishwomen who, unveiled and in most unfeminine garments, were talking and eating in the adjoining room with their lord and master. Almost unquestionably we were criticized, condemned, weighed in the balance and found wanting.

In India, after generations of living under the rule of the British Raj, the women, both Hindoo and Mussulman, have become familiar with the manners and customs of the Memsahib, have learned to understand, if not to concur with, the liberty that is hers. But in Algeria it is not so. The natural timidity of the average French-woman, and her dislike of discomfort, keeps her chained to the towns and prevents her from penetrating to the outlying districts of what, after all, is one of France's most valuable colonies, with the result that she is practically an unknown quantity to the native women of the country, and a European woman traveller is still a *rara avis* who is viewed with profound astonishment.

Nor is this disinclination to travel confined only to the female sex. There are hundreds of French-men doing business in the northern towns of Algeria, men who have lived all their lives in the country, who have never ventured even so far south as Touggourt—though there is a little rail-way to take them there—and who know nothing whatever of the desert.

And it is a country which would richly repay greater attention at the hands of its rulers. Even in the north the really valuable mineral deposits,

THE LATE MESSAOUD BEN AKLI AND SIDI LAI'D TIDJANI (ON RIGHT)

and other natural sources of wealth, are largely being developed by foreign capital—a fact I have heard deeply deplored by thinking Arabs of the better classes.

It was some two hours after lunch before our kind host would let us continue our journey. And when at last we got away we found that the mules and the riding camels had also been treated to a *large hospitalité*, so at first progress was very slow.

But to-day haste was not essential, and we were content to ride on slowly, glad to feel that the great start had really been made, and to enjoy quietly the surrounding country, which from now on was new to us.

South of Tamelhat lie ranges of sand dunes, smaller than those in the region of the Souf, but large enough to break the monotony of the landscape and to try out the climbing powers of the mules.

Clear of these the way became a fairly well-worn caravan track that led over undulating, sandy ground, past several small villages and one or two little oases of flourishing palm gardens. The villages had a deserted appearance, for the midday siesta was barely over and the majority of the inhabitants were still invisible. Only a few huddled bundles of humanity, lying like the sheeted dead outside the doors of their houses, raised sleepy heads to murmur a response to our greetings.

CAMPING IN THE SAHARA

The baggage camels had gone on without stopping at Tamelhat. Nor did we see them again until late in the afternoon, when, topping some rising ground, we caught sight of our first camp in process of erection about a mile away.

It was a very clear day, and the white tents, the unladen camels already scattering to crop the scanty herbage, and the little figures of the men running busily here and there, stood out in sharp relief against the background of the desert, but tiny, as though seen through the wrong end of a telescope.

Far off in the distance the tops of the palm trees of the oasis of Blidet-Amor were just visible, and a few miles away to the east the minaret of an abandoned village rose like a needlepoint into the evening sky. As always just before the setting of the sun, the colours were darkening and intensifying, the cloudless blue arch overhead turning from azure to ultramarine, the pale yellow of the sand deepening to saffron.

No longer was it necessary to urge the mules forward. The unaccustomed lunch was forgotten in the prospect of supper, and they rushed that last mile in record time.

Tents were all up when we arrived, the *maharist* who had joined us en route working with a will amongst our men, and at the entrance of the mess tent the indefatigable Kharbouch stood waving a teapot in welcome.

That first cup of tea after getting into camp is

the most eagerly-looked-for meal in the day. It was not often that we had to wait long for it. *Usually*, whenever it was possible and safe, the main part of the caravan, not resting in the middle of the day as we did, kept always a few miles ahead, so that when we reached camp at sunset the cook tent, at least, was up and the kettle boiling. There were times, of course, when, for some reason or another, we outstripped the baggage camels and had to wait. But happily it was a rare occurrence, for on these occasions abysmal gloom descended on our entourage, and heated recriminations took place when the caravan eventually drifted in, during which C. and I usually effaced ourselves and left them to it until peace was restored. And it was never very long. We would leave them wrangling and scowling as if they were ready to fly at each other's throats, but ten minutes later they would be laughing and shouting in perfect harmony again. Algerian Arabs are very like children, excitable, jealous, aud quick to take offence ; but they are thoughtful, trustworthy, and absolutely devoted when once they have given their affection.

But at this first camp there was no thought of trouble. Everything went with clock-like precision. The men were all accustomed to working together, most of them had travelled with us before and knew our ways and requirements. All our little personal fads had been remembered and attended to. And when, later, we went to our

sleeping tent, we found everything placed in the
order we liked, and it seemed hardly possible to
believe that two years had passed since they had
last set out our suit-cases and arranged the cots
with such methodical care.

That evening we dined early, for we were to
march in earnest the next day, with the flaps
of the mess tent wide open to the starry night.

And a couple of hours later, when the men had
fed, a big fire of brushwood was lighted before the
tent, and sitting collected about it, they gave us
a concert.

Staring for inspiration into the leaping flames,
Lakada piped plaintive little tunes full of odd
trills and shakes, accompanied by the rhythmical
beat of the tom-tom that sounded now loudly now
softly in Kharbouch's capable hands. First one
would sing and then another, the rest clapping
their hands to mark the time and joining in the
chorus—love songs, the songs of the nomad to his
camel, the songs of a wanderer on a journey, some
sad, some gay.

It was interesting to watch their faces, their
mobile features betraying the quick emotion that
stirred them ; to see their eyes kindle and droop,
their bodies sway gently to the lilt of the music.

Then, amidst encouraging shouts of " *Maama,
Maama,*" " the Sentimentalist " rose, smirking self-
consciously, to his feet and, knotting a handkerchief tightly about his slim waist, proceeded to
give a remarkably fine imitation of an Almée

performing one of the Ouled Nail dances, that reduced us all to helpless mirth. For his airs and graces, his ogling at his fellow cameleers, were such a ridiculous travesty of the real thing that when at last he collapsed sprawling full length on the sand we were weak from laughing, and could only feebly cheer him on to further efforts.

But by this time the fire had burnt down to a glowing mass of red embers, and, mindful of the early start next morning, we dismissed the men with a round of applause and reiterated " *Saheit, saheit*,—it is good, it is good," and, with a last look at the stars, turned in for the night.

II

HADJÏERA THE HAUNTED

THE sun was beating down fiercely out of a cloudless sky the day we arrived at Hadjïera, where we were to stay for a short visit with the Caid as his guests.

We had made an early start, hoping to reach our destination in time for lunch, but the heat was affecting the animals as well as ourselves, and we did not feel inclined to press forward over a route that was not easy going. A succession of low-spreading sand dunes, alternating with long stretches of rocky ground set thick with stones that ranged in size from tiny pebbles to huge boulders, kept us at a walking pace. The flies, too, were persistent and troublesome, and it was undoubtedly owing to them that here, for the only time on the trip, C.'s mule behaved badly. In one of the stony stretches, and in the worst possible place, where every hoof had to be set down with care, the animal suddenly leaped into the air, then began to bound violently backwards and forwards, kicking wildly, and jerking at the bridle. Two of the men urged their camels forward to head her should she bolt, but they dared not close in too nearly lest they should precipitate what we wanted to avoid. For the moment it looked as if she had gone mad, and I waited with my heart in my mouth, for a slip would have meant a bad accident. But at last C. managed to quiet her. And as there proved to be nothing wrong with her, we could only conclude that she had been severely stung by some insect, and watch out for further winged enemies.

Shortly after this we left the rocks behind and got into easier country, travelling over rising and falling ground, with a range of low hills on our left.

On the highest peaks of these hills are stone towers, set at a distance of about ten kilometres apart, erected to mark a known caravan route. These direction towers, built in a few instances by the French Government, but more usually by the various Caids through whose territory the trade routes run, are found in several other parts of the country, and are very useful when sandstorms or sudden floods sweep away all other indications of a track.

We had camped near some nomads the previous night, but this rocky stretch of country failing to supply even the scanty herbage that satisfies the desert flocks we saw no other sign of life until midday, when the scene grew somewhat less desolate and we began to overtake scattered bunches of camels grazing in charge of a solitary Arab or two.

CAMPING IN THE SAHARA

We were watching the antics of a band of youngsters—and baby camels play together exactly like lambs—gambolling ridiculously a little way ahead of us, when they suddenly scattered and fled in all directions. And looking for the cause of their alarm, we saw a *maharist* speeding towards us at an almost incredible pace. The *mahari* (riding camel), a slender, beautifully proportioned creature, was stretched out like a racehorse, while his rider, keeping his balance by what seemed only a miracle, was throwing his rifle up in the air and waving his arms like a lunatic.

Hardly slackening speed, he bore down on us, circling our little company two or three times before he came to a halt, to be greeted with roars of laughter and welcome by the men, who all knew him.

This maddest, merriest soul who ever enlivened a day's march proved to be Maama Xime, a tribesman and ex-*goumier* (Arab soldier) of the Caid of Hadjiera, who had been sent to escort us to his Chief's home.

We were later to become well acquainted with Maama Xime, for, many weeks afterwards, towards the end of the trip, he joined us at Ouargla and travelled with us back to Touggourt.

During that time he fully justified his reputation as being one of the most daring and accomplished camel riders in the country. There was nothing he could not do with a camel, and his handling of savage and untractable specimens was a wonder

THE DESERTED TOWN (HADJIERA)

that left even their owners gaping with astonishment. Agile as a cat, he rarely troubled to make his camel kneel when he mounted, but, burdened though he might be with a rifle and all kinds of odds and ends of impedimenta, would spring up on to the back of his *mahari*—already going at racing speed, for these riding camels go off like a shot the moment they are touched—and lie sprawling face downwards, squirming like an eel, until he could twist himself upright and gather his belongings into position, singing the while at the top of his voice. One of his special feats was a wild leap into the saddle which was exactly like the flying mount of the Western cowboy.

The Caid was expecting us to lunch, but as we had some distance yet to go and the heat was intense, we decided to lunch where we were and wait for an hour or two until it became cooler.

Unless we are travelling through country where it is advisable for the whole caravan to keep together, it is at the midday halt that the baggage camels, who march all day without resting, forge ahead and leave us and our personal attendants to follow, so that when we come up with them again in the evening we may find the night's camp in the process of erection. But we always keep with us a little tent, which is packed on the cook's camel, as a refuge from the sun during the siesta should there be no natural shelter available.

Sometimes on the march we would halt for

lunch at a *bordj*, or rest-house, a small domed building of two or three rooms opening on to a half-covered-in courtyard where the animals are stabled. These *bordjes* have usually a caretaker, but no food can be obtained and the rooms are unfurnished.

At other times, should a village be near, we would beg the loan of a palm garden from some cultivator for the midday siesta; then again, in rocky country, an overhanging cliff would give sufficient shelter. But to-day there was neither *bordj*, nor palm garden, nor shade of any kind. So the little tent was pitched, a couple of blankets were thrown down inside, and we crawled in out of the sun, while Kharbouch brought his saddle-bags and unpacked a cold lunch.

In the desert one eats enormously—when there is anything to eat—but there are limits to every-one's capacity. Kharbouch, a really fine cook and jealous of his reputation, would not admit this, and scolded us soundly if there was not a clean sweep made at every meal. It was over the dinners, when he had more time for preparation, that he gave full rein to his culinary skill, and he never let us off with less than four courses, and that even when provisions and the wood to cook with were hard to come by. To him dinner was not a mere meal, but a solemn rite, over which he declined to hurry, and sometimes, from one cause or another, it was long past nine o'clock before we heard his rather pompous voice announcing that the soup was served. But the result was always worth waiting for. Often we used to drift into the cook tent to watch him at his work, and, unlike some cooks, he always made us welcome. Divested of burnous and gandoura, with his shirt sleeves rolled up to the elbow, his turban tipped rakishly at the back of his head, the inevitable cigarette drooping from the corner of his mouth, he would sit cross-legged before the brushwood fire, bending over the iron grid that was all his cooking stove, daintily manipulating a dozen pots and pans while he kept an admiring audience in roars of laughter at his jokes.

It was still very hot when we packed up and pushed on towards Hadjïera.

Sand dunes began again almost immediately, and for a couple of hours we plodded over them, until it seemed almost impossible that we could escape from the labyrinth in which we found ourselves. Hemmed in by the dunes, there was nothing to see but the next sandy hillock to be surmounted, and nothing to break the monotony except the invariable race for lead that took place between C.'s mule and mine as they ploughed down each shifting, sliding slope.

At last by degrees the dunes grew smaller and wider apart, open spaces began to appear and then attempts at cultivation—a group of palm trees here and there, then more palms, and patches of barley—until we were winding up a steep hillside that was set thick with tiny gardens.

CAMPING IN THE SAHARA

On the ridge of the hill we stood for a moment to breathe the beasts, and, looking down over a large plain, saw Hadjïera straggling out below us.

The old town, which is now deserted except for the priests, stands on slightly rising ground about a quarter of a mile from the Caid's palace. Dotted over the plain lie clusters of minute villages—to each village a family—and well-cultivated palm and vegetable gardens.

The Caid was waiting on the terrace of his palace with his entourage grouped around him, and as we drew nearer he ran down the stone staircase to meet us.

Mohammed Seghir ben Smail, Caid des Said-Ouled-Amor, Chevalier of the Legion of Honour, and chief of three big tribes, is one of the finest examples of native ruler. Intelligent and progressive, an indefatigable worker, kindly and sympathetic, he governs his tribes with a rod of iron, but also with a high sense of justice, and is worshipped by his people.

Nothing could have been kinder than his welcome, and his hospitality during our stay was unending.

The baggage camels had got in some time before, and our tents were already pitched a few yards away from the palace. Mint tea appeared at once, and for a while we sat on the cool, shady terrace sipping the customary three glasses, while the Caid plied us with questions and, himself

MOHAMMED SEGHIR BEN SMAIL, CAID OF HADJIERA

thoroughly at ease, made us feel completely at home before five minutes had passed.

Here, too, was seen the real democracy of the East, for not only we, but our personal attendants also were received on the terrace and, at a decorous distance from ourselves, supplied with tea and sugar cakes.

After we were rested and his entourage had been presented the Caid suggested a visit to the old town.

So under his guidance we set off, and for more than an hour wandered through the deserted streets and houses of old Hadjïera.

Built at a time when the tribes of that district were perpetually at war, it stands in a commanding position on a rocky hill, and encircled by a fortified wall, it must in those old days have been an almost impregnable stronghold. But with the three adjacent tribes gathered now peaceably under one head the need for a fortress is past, and the wall is fast falling into disrepair. Although it has been abandoned for a number of years, the town looks as if the inhabitants had walked out only yesterday. Most of the buildings are intact and still remain perfectly habitable, though here and there one has collapsed into ruins, blocking the narrow streets with a mass of stones and rubble that can only be scrambled over with difficulty. But this is no more than is found, particularly after an extra wet season, in many another town still populated and busy.

CAMPING IN THE SAHARA

The real reason for the abandonment of old Hadjïera was difficult to discover, and in view of the evasive answers received in reply to direct questions—for the true Arab is always loath to admit what he prefers to withhold—I am not sure that the ultimate explanation at which I arrived in my own mind is not more than a glimmering of the real truth.

That the present Caid, with his modern and advanced ideas, should have desired a larger and more commodious residence than the rather cramped quarters in the middle of the old town which satisfied all the requirements of his forbears is understandable; but that his subjects should have deserted their ancient dwellings and followed him out beyond the city walls to form new homes for a mere whim is less easy to credit. The water supply of the town did not fail, nor did any strange disease sweep through the crowded streets and decimate the inhabitants.

Not until we reached the open space that was the old market-place did I begin to understand that perhaps a subtler, more " intriguing " reason than I had yet imagined was the cause of the general exodus from the town. For the market-place of old Hadjïera is haunted, and no man ventures into it now after nightfall.

There is no visible manifestation, no djinn or afreet appears in horrible guise to rob men of their senses, but the brave mortal who dares to invade the spirit's sanctuary—and no mortal of the neigh-

THE HAUNTED MARKET-PLACE, HADJIERA

hourhood is found willing to dare in these days—
is greeted with showers of stones thrown by invisible hands, which fusillade is kept up until the
rash visitor departs.   In his youth the Caïd himself
made the experiment, and met with the usual
reception.   And while he told me that no power on
earth would induce him to undergo the experience
again, he was most anxious that I, as a foreigner
and immune from local superstition, should make
a visit to the market-place after dark and try my
luck.   But since this involved going alone, for
which I am not ashamed to own I had no fancy,
and because I am too Scotch to deny the super-
natural, I begged to be excused.

Even in the daytime there is something in the
atmosphere of certain portions of the old town
that is disquieting, that makes one glance furtively
over one's shoulder, and step aside hastily where
no tangible obstruction can be seen.

The mosque is still used, and is in good repair ;
but of all the old inhabitants only the priests and
their families remain, crowded together like rabbits
in a warren in a big crumbling building perched
high up on the city wall.

And without being sceptical, I was moved to
wonder what part sacerdotalism has played, and
is still playing, in the growth of superstition that
has left to the priesthood the sole occupation of
old Hadjïera.

Statistics make it impossible to deny the spread
of Islam, but it is an Islamism that is shorn of

much of its former fanaticism. In Algeria, as in other Mohammedan countries, it is very obvious that the old order of things is changing, giving place to the new. Year by year closer contact with the outside world is producing a certain broader-mindedness and a wider outlook on life among the upper classes that is tending to promote intellectualism and foster individual independence of thought, and more and more is religion being relegated to the masses. There are, of course, many left amongst the higher social grades who still cling tenaciously to the stricter tenets of their faith. But it is more generally among the humbler followers of the Prophet that one finds the old unquestioning belief, and the closer and more frequent attention to ceremonial practice.

The Mohammedan priesthood is facing the same problem that is disturbing the ministers of all Churches throughout the world: gradually but surely its absolute ascendancy over the minds of its adherents in matters spiritual and temporal is being undermined, and it is falling from its high estate of supremacy into a position of secondary importance. And seeing their power going from them, small wonder that a certain section of the priests seek to re-establish their prestige by any and every means possible, even, as perhaps in the case of Hadjïera, by playing on the superstitious fears of a still credulous people. I say a certain section advisedly, for there are among the heads of the various Mohammedan sects in Algeria men

OUR STAFF

Names reading from left to right. *Standing:*—BEN HAOUR, MAAMA XIME, HAMA SEGHIR, MAAMA THE "SENTIMENTALIST."
Sitting:— MOHAMED, KHARBOUCH, LAKADA

of great intelligence and education, who must realize that the days of blind credulity are drawing to an end, and that Islamism, if it is to continue, must continue along more modern and progressive lines.

It is not among the highly placed marabouts that one finds the pretended miracle-worker or the furious fanatic.

Among other buildings in old Hadjïera which are still in perfect repair is the ancestral home of the Caid, where he too lived as a young man. Very small are the rooms, and very steep and narrow the stairways leading to the upper chambers.

Close inside the main entrance, and immediately adjoining the suite of rooms that were set apart for the harem, is a small ante-room or guard-room, in a recess of which the Caid's favourite charger was stabled and, in the old turbulent days, kept saddled day and night in case of emergency.

Beneath the ground floor, and reached by a flight of almost precipitous steps, range a vault-like set of apartments with low arched roofs supported by massive stone pillars. Here the whole family retired in the summertime, for then the heat in Hadjïera is intense. Almost completely dark, it must have been a gloomy habitation, and an unpleasantly crowded one, for chiefs usually gather about them not only their own immediate families, but also kinsmen to any degree of relationship; while servants, both Arab and negro, abound.

This habit, which was almost universal, of going to ground to avoid the summer heat is still practised by some of the more conservative of the older people, and all about the environs of Hadjïera are found cave-like dwellings tunnelled out of the hard sandstone which forms the sub-soil.

Hadjïera possesses one feature which makes it unique among the old Arab towns of Algeria. Set in the heart of the city are two public latrines, primitive in construction but quite adequate, and supplied with an underground drainage system that is not found anywhere else in the country, except in one or two of the Mozabite towns, where the principal streets have sewers that show a distinct Roman influence.

The rock on which old Hadjïera is built is in places badly weathered, full of deep fissures and honeycombed with cavities. In one of these cavities, reaching far back into the rock, lived a peculiarly holy man, long since dead, who in his lifetime exerted a very great influence over Hadjïera and its people. Once the dominant power of the neighbourhood, it may be perhaps his restless spirit that haunts the market-place so effectually to-day.

From the old town the Caid, full of energy and enthusiasm, led us for an extensive tour amongst the adjacent palm gardens and vegetable plots.

Water being plentiful here, cultivation abounds and grains of various kinds, barley, carrots and beans, grow freely. Each vegetable plot is screened round with a hedge of dried palm fronds to keep back the ever-encroaching sand, and each has its own well to supply the constant irrigation that is necessary to ensure a good crop.

The water, drawn from the well in skin buckets, is first emptied into a big shallow trough of hard earth, and from there finds its way through little intersecting canals all over the garden. Sometimes these buckets are drawn up by hand. But usually a camel, or more often a mule, is harnessed to the tackling over the well, and spends a monotonous existence plodding backwards and forwards along the narrow runway that is worn and grooved with the passage of many feet. All day long this irrigation is going on, and in the neighbourhood of an oasis the most constant and dominating sounds are the whine and scream of the well ropes and the cries of the gardeners as they call to their patient beasts.

At Hadjïera the water is very little below the level of the ground, and the palm trees are planted in deep pits dug out of the hard sandstone, so that their roots may reach down to the moisture that is essential to their growth.

This excavation entails hard work, as we were able to see for ourselves, for the Caid, anxious to show all there was of interest in his domain, and himself a very powerful man, seized a pickaxe lying near and toiled valiantly for a full five minutes to demonstrate the labours of his people. Then, laughing like a boy, he hoisted up his heavy burnous, thrust his hands into the pockets of his wide trousers, and ran up the steep embankment at a pace we were hard put to follow.

Still talking, he escorted us back to our tents, where we in turn played host and gave him some English-made tea, which he thought peculiarly nasty, though he was too polite to say so.

After an exhaustive inspection of the whole camp he left us, recommending " a little repose " before the time came to join him for dinner at the palace.

But there was not much time for rest, for we still had to unpack and make ourselves presentable for the evening.

Personal baggage having of necessity been cut down to the minimum, we could not do much in the matter of toilet, and a clean shirt was all we could achieve in honour of the festive occasion. But at least our coats were brushed speckless and boots polished until they shone. Yet even these slight preparations were scarcely concluded before a genial shout outside the tent announced our host, come himself to escort us through the darkness.

It was a beautiful night, still and windless, and refreshingly cool after the heat of the day.

Following the Caid, who had a lighted lantern swinging in his hand, we stumbled over the rough

THE CAID'S PALACE

ground towards the palace, where a single shaft of light issued from an open doorway on the terrace.

On our left the dark, irregular mass of the abandoned town towered gloomy and sinister-looking against the skyline, and there was a suggestion of creepiness in the air that made any strange happening seem possible.

But from the eerie solitude of the night we passed into a brilliantly lit room, where the bustle of preparation and a babel of voices quickly banished all thought of spooks.

The reception-room is a large oblong apartment, more French than Arab in general appearance. A dining-table, a writing bureau—at which Mohammed Seghir and his secretary spend several hours each day working at business connected with his large territory and his numerous commercial enterprises—a sofa, a couple of easy chairs, and the inevitable gramophone, make up all the furnishings, and leave plenty of space to move about.

On the whitewashed walls hang trophies and a few photographs ; while the floor is covered, as in other rooms in the house, with beautiful rugs designed by the Caid himself in the Kairouan style and made for him at Guémar in the Souf.

There was a slight delay in serving dinner, and it was somewhat of a shock to learn that we were waiting for our hostess ! I knew Mohammed Seghir to be broad-minded and progressive in his ideas, but this apparent violation of custom seemed beyond the bounds of all possibility. But I might have known better, and Mohammedan scruples were fated not to be outraged—for our hostess was but four years of age, the Caid's niece and constant companion.

A most engaging little person, quaintly dressed in a long mauve satin gown and with a sequinned cap perched coquettishly on the side of her tiny head, she came, gravely shy but wondrously polite, to clutch her uncle's hand and gaze at the strangers with round eyes of wonder. But for all her shyness an intelligent mite, who, once told, made no mistake as to which was Madame and which Mademoiselle, and her table manners were perfect. That she was the pet of the whole household was obvious, for we had to wait for our soup until she was firmly settled on the pile of cushions placed on her chair, and her dinner napkin tied under her chin by a burly negro who was evidently her adoring slave.

Valiantly she wrestled with a tiny portion of each course, but the hour was late and the meal protracted, and the little head began at length to droop and the bright eyes to grow heavier and heavier. Time and again she would almost drop off, then wake abruptly to smile confidingly at the Caid and pat his hand with a cooing murmur of " *Sidi*," that showed where was all her young affection. It became apparent that the claims of society would have to give place to the claims

THE CAID AND HIS LITTLE NIECE

of the sandman. And at last the Caïd, who had drawn her on to his knee, gave her into the arms of the big negro and she was carried off to bed, waving her hand and still smiling seraphically. But she was fast asleep before they reached the door.

We sat on at the table far into the night, talking of Algeria, of the proposed route of our trip—which route was that night fated to be completely changed, for it was the Caïd of Hadjïera who persuaded me to abandon my original intention of going west after leaving Ghardaia in the M'Zab Valley, and to make instead for El-Goléa in the south—and of affairs international in general.

From affairs international we came by natural sequence to affairs internal, and again I was asked the question that many other Algerian Arabs have put to me—How does the French administration of Algeria compare with the British rule in India ? It is a subject that has to be approached delicately, and not one that can be enlarged upon here. Conversation drifted eventually, as it must always with Arabs, to commerce and trade.

The season of sheep shearing was drawing near, and the Caïd, who, besides owning innumerable date palms, is rich in flocks and herds, had much to say of the wool-clip not only of Algeria, but also of all the wool-producing countries of the world. It was interesting to hear him glibly enumerating the principal centres of the wool trade in England, but we felt bound to protest when he asserted the independence of Australia. Politely but firmly we claimed the great southern continent as part of the British Empire.

The Caid pushed back his chair and stared at us aghast. " You have Canada and India, and Allah only knows how much of Africa. But Australia also—is it possible ? "

When we convinced him that it was not only possible but true, he banged his hand on the table and roared with laughter. " *Awā, awā,* you English," he exclaimed, " you own the world ! "

With all due modesty we set a limit to the boundaries of our Empire, and for the rest of the evening discoursed on geography to satisfy the Caid's insatiable thirst for information.

The next morning we were able to luxuriate in an extra hour of bed and a leisurely rising. Usually it was a case of scrambling, still half asleep, into one's clothes, and a hasty packing of suit-cases, conscious all the time that the rest of the camp was already packed up and the men were hovering about outside ready to tear down the tent the moment we emerged.

It was another brilliant day, calm and clear, and C. spent some time photographing.

When I first visited Algeria, as a child, it was almost impossible to get any rigid Mohammedan to face the camera. But time has changed that. Nowadays not only chiefs and marabouts of high standing, but also the general populace pose for their portraits readily and with enthusiasm.

The Caid proved to be a capital subject, his only regret being that we had not brought a cinematograph apparatus with us. And the talk turning on moving pictures, we told him how, when travelling some time ago in the Souf near El-Oued, we had stopped to camp one evening outside a village where the inhabitants, who had formed part of the crowd for certain scenes in the famous French film "L'Atlantide," thinking that we too must be a cinema troupe, had come to us en masse, hoping to be taken on as supers. Which story the Caid capped by informing us that in him we saw a genuine film actor; that other scenes of "L'Atlantide" had been taken, with his permission, at Hadjïera; and that he himself, with his secretary as second-in-command, had charged at the head of his own troops in the great battle scene. He was much amused that the film company had insisted on wooden swords and spears being used, and showed us some spirited photographs of his troops rehearsing for the picture.

Later in the morning the Caid most kindly escorted us through his house, where, in a charming suite of rooms, we had the pleasure of meeting his wife.

Not yet emancipated, Arab ladies still employ their leisure in spinning and weaving, and it was interesting to see the bundles of fine wool and hanks of black and brown camel hair arranged for use, and to watch burnouses and gandouras in process of manufacture.

The house is far bigger than it outwardly appears, and is built round three separate courtyards open to the air. From the principal courtyard, that of the private apartments, a stone stairway leads to a kind of rampart, from which a wide view of the surrounding country is obtained. The third courtyard, where are the kitchens, is given over to the domestic staff, which is numerous and consists of both Arabs and negroes. Here also are the married servants' quarters, each with its own separate entrance door opening from without to ensure the domestic privacy that the Mohammedan religion demands.

Leaving the house by way of the kitchen courtyard, we stopped for a moment to watch the cooking of the *meshwe* which was to form the *pièce de résistance* that day at lunch.

A *meshwe*, which is a national dish among the Arabs, and given only when special honour is shown to a guest, is a sheep roasted whole over the embers of a wood fire, and so brought to table, where it is eaten with the fingers, as the touch of steel is supposed to destroy the fine flavour. Originally no Mohammedan, following the Prophet's order, would use steel to cut any food, but this is one of the strict observances not adhered to nowadays.

Cooking a *meshwe* is an exhausting business.

THE CAID AND HIS ENTOURAGE

Killed and cleaned, the sheep is immediately spitted with a stout stake thrust through the whole length of the body. Two men grasp the ends of the stake and hold the carcase over the glowing embers, revolving it continually, while others stand by to baste, first with salt and water, then with a kind of liquid butter. Since the *meshwe* must be cooked for at least two hours, relays of cooks are needed, for the heat from the wood embers is intense and twenty minutes is as much as a man can stand at a time.

But the result is worth waiting for, and that particular *meshwe* is an abiding remembrance.

It came at last—after many previous courses that left us wondering how we were to do justice to the ceremonious dish prepared in our honour and yet have sufficient energy left to ride during the afternoon—looking very like the Paschal lamb with its head and its heels and the appurtenances thereof, and was set down on the middle of the table on a flat board.

Urged on by the Caid, himself a valiant trencherman, we plunged our fingers into the succulent flesh, and ate until we could eat no more. Eastern custom demands that a guest shows due appreciation of the food placed before him, and lack of appetite is regarded as an insult. We had the honour of England to uphold, and we upheld it—but it was a bare fifteen kilometres we accomplished that afternoon after leaving Hadjïera.

CAMPING IN THE SAHARA

Arabs have ways of dispensing hospitality which are somewhat disconcerting to Occidentals possessed of any sense of humour. It is, for instance, difficult to preserve one's own gravity when a grave, earnest host, eager to do the honours of his table, plucks some special tit-bit from the savoury carcase and, rolling it into a ball, himself conveys it into one's mouth. One can only accept, choke a mumbled thanks, and avoid the eyes of one's fellow sufferers.

It was not easy to escape from our kind and hospitable host. He was most keen that we should remain on for at least a week as his guests, and sketched an elaborate programme of sport and amusement that was almost too tempting to resist. But the alteration in our route involving a much longer journey in the desert than had originally been planned, we were forced to push on, and left Hadjïera the Haunted with many mutual regrets.

III

THE MOZABITES

VERY little is still known of the Mozabites, or M'Zabi, that peculiar people who, five or six hundred years ago, revolting against certain tenets of the Mohammedan faith, broke away from their co-religionists and marched out into the wilderness to found new homes where they might practise in peace the modified form of Islamism that has to-day earned them the name of the Protestant Mohammedans.

That they eventually reached and established themselves in the Valley of the M'Zab, situated in the heart of a wild mountainous region about one hundred miles south of Lagouat, and there multiplied and prospered, is common knowledge. But what started the new movement, what were the precise causes that led to this great break-away, and who actually were their leaders is still wrapped in mystery.

No reliable history of the Mozabites has yet been written. The few pamphlets on the subject which have appeared, French for the most part, are contradictory and in some cases entirely erroneous, according to local Arab information I was lucky enough to obtain.

The Mozabites are a remnant of the original Berber stock who held the country before the coming of the Arabs in A.D. 647. Their facial characteristics and the architectural adornment of their buildings go to prove this.

A race apart, they differ from their neighbours not only in matters of religion, but also in manners and customs and certain peculiarities in dress. Endowed with greater abilities than the average Arab, their general mentality is considerably in advance of other tribes in Algeria, except perhaps the Kabyles, and in the main they still preserve the same courage, resourcefulness and tenacity of purpose that drove them out into the wilderness so many hundreds of years ago.

At first it was a fight for mere existence. Having found in the desolate, inaccessible region of the M'Zab the sure refuge they sought, they built there seven heavily fortified towns, erected watch-towers on the hilltops at the head of the passes leading to the valley, and sat down to defy their enemies.

In process of time, by grim determination and perseverance, they transformed the bare and inhospitable valley into a succession of rich and flourishing oases.

The Mozabites are skilled in building and have rather more than an elementary knowledge of hydraulics, and their towns—Ghardaia, M'lika,

THE MOZABITES

Ben Isguen, El-Atteuf, Bounoura, Berrian and Guerrara—are planned with more attention to detail than is common in Arab towns and have, beside a more than usually abundant water supply, a system of street drainage which, though simple, is most effective.

Their mosques, too, have a feature which is peculiar and interesting. The top of the minaret, where the *muezzin* stands to call the faithful to prayer, is not open as in other Mohammedan mosques, but is built in the shape of a cone, with four narrow lateral slits, facing the cardinal points of the compass, through which the *muezzin* projects his voice. Cut off in this way from the sight of all worldly happenings beneath him, it is thought that the *muezzin* has a better chance of keeping his mind free from mundane matters, and of concentrating more fully on holy thought and his priestly vocation.

The Valley of the M'Zab was annexed by France in 1882. But the Mozabites have their own ideas on this annexation and have resolutely refused military service, for they maintain that they only signed a treaty of alliance.

The French have built large barracks at Ghardaia, the principal town, but the garrison numbers only a very few men of a Soudanese regiment under a French Commandant. Guerrara, also, has a Bureau Arabe, supposed to be in charge of a French lieutenant, but actually operated by a Mozabite. And the civil administration of the district still remains in the hands of the inhabitants.

The Mozabites have a system of federal government.

Each town elects a Council of Twelve, who themselves elect a central Council of Twelve which sits at Ghardaia, and to which the lesser councils refer any disputed matter for final settlement. In bygone years this Supreme Council at Ghardaia used to meet in the market-place, where they sat on twelve white stones, which are still to be seen. Nowadays their meetings are conducted more privately in a Council Chamber.

Set over each town, and working with the Councils of Twelve, is a Caid.

These Mozabite Caids are not, as amongst other Arabs, hereditary princes, but are men of special worth and ability who are elected by their fellow townsmen to watch over their interests and take the lead in municipal affairs. Combining as they do the functions of chief magistrate, registrar, general trade adviser and director of tariffs, these Caids would seem to have unique opportunity for personal enrichment, were it not for the fact that they hold their office only by virtue of their integrity. For though they are normally elected for life, they can still be deposed if they abuse their power, or their honesty be proved to be doubtful. But this is a rare happening, and the majority are said to be scrupulous, hard-working men who have the interests of the community at heart, and who benefit in no way by their high position.

An industrious and prosperous people, the Mozabites are famous as traders. This commercial instinct leads them far afield through all the Barbary States, where they establish shops and business houses and work until they have amassed a sufficient fortune to enable them to return to the M'Zab, when their places abroad are taken by other members of the family.

But even though this absence may extend over years, their wives and children are left at home. In consequence the Mozabite women enjoy a greater freedom than is usual amongst Mohammedan females. Left for long periods alone, they are forced to take the place of absent husbands and fathers, and to buy and sell and conduct affairs that otherwise would be entirely in the hands of their menkind. That they make good is probably due to the fact that they have a certain amount of education, for amongst the Mozabites girls as well as boys must attend school. In this they resemble the Touareg women of the Hoggar Mountains, who are also left much alone—though their husbands are bandits and not traders—and who are reported to be exceptionally intelligent, combining shrewd business abilities with a pretty taste in verse-making.

Besides trading, the Mozabites are skilled craftsmen, specializing in cabinet work, the finished articles being painted with fantastic designs in rather glaring colours — leather work, basket-making and embroidery.

Family life in the M'Zab is said to be happy, and the children are usually serious, well-conducted little mortals. There is possibly a reason for this, for the naughty child has always hanging over his or her head the fear of the Children's Court, with its formidable Council of Elders.

When a boy or girl is proved to be beyond parental control, the last resort is this Children's Court, where the youthful offender is tried and judged, the boys by men, the girls by women.

The trial is a very solemn and serious business. Most formally conducted, with a counsel for the prosecution and a counsel for the defence, it must be a big ordeal for the shivering little sinner— probably not so wicked, after all, if judged by our standards—brought to face the awe-inspiring array of grim city fathers, or mothers as the case may be, who are judge and jury rolled into one. The fear of these trials is said to be a great deterrent to juvenile indiscretion, and the results, though corporal punishment is never administered, both satisfactory and lasting.

With regard to other religions, the Mozabites are very tolerant. At Ghardaia, for example, besides their own places of worship, there is a mosque for orthodox Mohammedans, and two large Jewish synagogues, while the Roman Catholic order of White Fathers have a big establishment—though few scholars, and those for the main part orthodox Arabs or negroes. Very occasionally a Mozabite, with an eye to the future, will send his son to learn from them what may be useful to him in business later on, but it is said the White Fathers have not yet made a single convert from amongst the M'Zabi.

Guerrara, least known and by far the most interesting, was the first Mozabite town we visited. A day's journey south of Hadjïera we left the Erg, or sandy country, and entered the Hamada, or rocky region.

'Very wild and desolate is this district of the Hamada, and for days we travelled over rough and difficult ground, seeing only occasionally a few starved-looking nomads, while we mounted steadily up towards the high plateaux.

Winding, scrambling, we pushed on as fast as possible, and that was not very fast when all is said, through narrow defiles and gulleys, down into steep, basin-like depressions, and up again to the bleak tableland that seemed to stretch in unbroken flatness for miles, but yet was full of slits and gashes that had to be nogotiated, so that often we rode three kilometres to make one.

Rising in places to over 2000 ft., swept at certain seasons of the year by a biting wind that cuts like a knife, these high plateaux, with their wide outlook and apparently level surface, form the only stretches of country in Algeria which, to my mind, can really be called monotonous. Just a waste of cold grey rock, pitiless and unyielding, tiresome to the eyes and cruel to travel over.

Here camping is a forlorn and chilly affair; and here, for the first time, we blessed the foresight which had provided iron tent pegs—for wooden ones would have been less than useless. As it was, one night, when it blew a young gale, we feared that even the iron pegs would not hold the straining canvas of our sleeping tent, and time and again the men came to beat them in further and tighten the ropes.

From the high Hamada we dropped suddenly several hundred feet, to begin climbing again through tortuous ravines shut in by long ranges of hills, whose jagged peaks were weathered into every conceivable shape and form. And now the rocks had changed in colour from grey to blood red that seemed to glow sombrely as if from an inward fire.

Mounting steadily upward, we came at last to a narrow winding pass. Hemmed in by tall cliffs, we urged the beasts over rough stony ground, that was like the dry bed of an old torrent, towards an opening in the cliff face. Behind us the men were shouting at the stumbling camels, tightening a rope here, adjusting a slipping load there, and skipping like goats from rock to rock as they rounded up the straggling caravan.

Totally unprepared for what was coming, our mules struggling as always for the foremost place, C. and I rode up the last few yards of the steep

OUR CAMP OUTSIDE GUERRARA

ascent, reached the narrow opening in the cliffs simultaneously—and almost cried out at the sheer beauty of the scene that opened before us. I think our feelings must have been very much like those of Moses when he looked down from the heights of Pisgah over the Promised Land.

Far below, in a huge valley enclosed by blood-red hills, lay Guerrara, almost unbelievably beautiful.

For days we had travelled through stark grey barrenness, through waterless ways and arid desolation. But here were light and colour and a mass of vegetation that, by contrast, was startling.

It was not the fortified town itself we saw, but the garden suburb that stretches for a mile and more beyond the city gates.

And for long we looked, unable to tear our eyes away. Tiny white buildings—summer resorts and gardeners' cottages—were grouped thickly, glistening like silver in the clear afternoon light; while all around them clustered patches of growing crops, vivid splashes of brightest green, above which rose the dark feathery mass of thousands of palm trees.

Slowly we rode down the long slope into the valley, hearing as we drew nearer the familiar creaking whine of well tacklings, the doleful bray of some disgruntled ass, the cheery laughter of busy field workers.

As we went I noticed what I thought was an orange lying beside the track, then another and

another, until the way was strewn with them.
Thinking some careless trader had spilled his load,
I asked the men if Guerrara was so rich in oranges
that they could pave the roads with them. With
a grin Lakada, the irrepressible, retrieved a big
one and tossed it up to me. Round and juicy-
looking, with a smooth yellow skin, it was exactly
like an orange, and I slipped it into my pocket
saying I would keep it for dinner. There was a
howl of laughter, and then I learned—though not
before C. and I had been laden down with dozens
—that this orange-like fruit is not an orange, but
a fungus growth which is highly poisonous. Nor
is it found on a tree or shrub. Fully grown in
its skin, it thrusts up out of the sandy ground
without leaf or root, though some have tiny
pendulous fibres.

The joke, of course, was too good to be left,
and all the way in to Guerrara the men, perfect
children at heart, kept handing them up until we
were forced to retaliate and pelt them with the
useless things.

Past innumerable gardens we rode, and then,
skirting the angle of a dense palm grove, saw
Guerrara rising before us.

The fortress town is built on a low hill, which
it completely covers, and is surrounded by a double
wall, the outer one having several gateways which
in the old turbulent times were also fortified
watch-towers.

We pitched our camp under the shelter of the

THE WALLED CITY OF GUERRARA

crimson cliffs just outside the city walls, and close to the tomb of a local holy man, who was kind enough not to disturb our slumbers by any nocturnal rambling.

Down in the valley the heat was intense, unusually so for the season, and until the sun went down we were glad to lie on the sand and watch the tents going up and the camels unloaded.

It was here that, for the first time, I saw camels eating bones—and bones, I regret to say, of their own kind. Eating them, too, with relish. Ours had a feast that afternoon, for all about the camp the ground was strewn with bare white ribs and huge leg bones, which they munched greedily. Even the babies joined in, and we saw Diavolo prance past with a colossal rib many sizes too big for him sticking out of his mouth.

After tea we pulled ourselves together and went to have a preliminary look at the town.

Somewhere among the maze of buildings there was a marriage festival in progress, and the sound of tom-toms and pipes came now softly, now loudly, as we wandered up and down the narrow, winding streets. Weird intermittent music it was, full of quarter tones and strange halts, barbaric and typically native. There is no haste about an Arab wedding, and when we turned in that night the tom-toms were still beating furiously, the pipes still blaring out their discordant blasts. Next morning we made an early start.

CAMPING IN THE SAHARA

Our first call was on the Caid, who received us in his office, plied us with the usual mint tea, and set himself to make polite conversation. But he was painfully shy, being unaccustomed to Europeans, and conversation would have languished on his side had it not been for Si A. S., who came to his rescue and gently but firmly kept him to the topics on which we wanted information.

His office was a bare little whitewashed room on the first floor of the house, reached by a precipitous stairway. The most interesting feature of the room was a large board, hung on the wall, covered with minute writing that proved to be a scale of the current market prices of the district.

Throughout our visit the Caid's secretary sat at a table piled with ledgers and notebooks apparently immersed in calculations. But I am afraid we entirely upset the routine of the office, for the columns of figures remained unadded and not a word did the secretary write. It was odd, too, how many of the city worthies found it imperative to consult their chief magistrate that morning! They arrived by ones and twos, babbled a few words, their eyes glued on our intriguing selves, and slipped away again—doubtless to discuss us for hours over mint tea and dominoes. Whenever Algerian Arabs have a few moments of leisure they play dominoes, and since the Prophet forbade gambling, they compromise by making the loser pay for the tea.

THE MARKET-PLACE AT GUERRARA

Before leaving, the Caid took us up to the roof of his house, from where we had a beautiful view of the surrounding country.

We went next to visit the French Government School.

The French have instituted these schools in all the big towns, and some of the smaller ones, in Algeria, though not farther south than the M'Zab Valley.

But though education is nominally supposed to be compulsory, actually it is not. And the French have as yet no means of enforcing it.

In many cases the school-houses are inadequate ; and masters, Kabyles for the main part, are not always forthcoming. At Guerrara, for instance, where there are hundreds of children—to put it at a low figure—only thirty can be accommodated in the little, ill-lit room that serves as the Government school. The remaining children of the town attend the Mozabite schools.

The education given in the Government schools is of necessity very elementary, for the boys leave while they are still quite young and rarely get past the primer stage.

In fairness to the French Government it must be added that in the big towns in the north of Algeria a little more attention is paid to the schools, but even in these there is scant encouragement given to the specially intellectual boy of the masses who wishes to rise to higher standards. It is only the sons of chiefs and rich men who can pass on, if they so wish, to the *lycées* and colleges in the north of the country.

We spent some time chatting with the school-master of Guerrara, a keen young Kabyle, and examining the children's reading-books and copies. The primers were of the Cat-sat-on-the-Mat variety, and that day the class was wrestling with the adventures of a pious youth named Pierre, who "was very kind to animals," which, in a land where animal suffering goes unnoticed, struck us as being somewhat humorous, and led one to wonder what the infant native mind made of it all.

Afterwards we thoroughly explored the steep, winding streets we had imperfectly seen in the twilight the night before, and C. took a number of photographs.

Visitors are very rare in Guerrara, and wherever we went we had a following tailing at our heels, which at times made photography difficult. But it was a friendly following, who seemed pleased to see us and anxious to do the honours of the town.

Later in the day we went to have tea with the Mozabite official in charge of the Bureau Arabe. He welcomed us in a long narrow apartment tastefully arranged with only Arab furnishings, amongst which were some fine old nail-studded wooden chests.

The room was deliciously cool after the heat and dust of the town.

The preliminary compliments over, we went out to a pretty little walled garden, where tea and

MOZABITES AT GUERRARA

cakes were waiting under the shade of some gnarled old fig trees.

When it grew cooler our host took us for a long tour through the lovely gardens that lie beyond the city gates. At the time of our visit the crops were well forward, and we passed from garden to garden, under a canopy of date palms, seeing barley, beans, carrots and onions, all apparently growing in rich profusion, as well as many other vegetables and grains whose names I did not know.

The Mozabite system of irrigation is much more complicated and advanced than in other parts of the country, and they make use of storage tanks for times of drought that are quite elaborate in design. The whole water question is a science to which the Mozabites have given much thought and unending labour.

Some distance up the valley, about half a mile beyond the garden suburb, they have built a wide barrage with several sluice gates, to control the M'Zab river when it comes down in spate, as it does every eight or ten years after an exceptional rainfall.

The sight must be magnificent, and rather awe-inspiring. For the flooded M'Zab, swollen by torrential rains and fed by hundreds of little streams rushing from the hills, pours down the valley at tremendous speed like a solid wall, feet high.

Before the building of the barrage it used to

sweep the valley right up to the city walls, drowning the gardens and doing damage that took years to repair. Now the great mass of water when it comes is held in check, and diverted gradually for the needs of the cultivators.

But this year, for all their storage tanks, the people were far from easy in their minds. Though, to our inexperienced eyes, the gardens appeared to be well watered, many cisterns were almost empty and many conduits had ceased to run. It was the second year of drought, and not only the Mozabites, but all Algeria was praying for rain.

As we stood on the top of the barrage looking up the length of the long, dry river-bed, it was difficult to believe that, almost without warning and in the space of a few hours, it could be transformed into a deep, raging torrent that would carry death and destruction in its path.

We little knew, that afternoon, how soon the Arabs' prayers were to be answered and how, incidentally, it was to affect ourselves.

The extension of our trip having made time a consideration, we could only afford to stay two days in Guerrara. Two months could be spent there with enjoyment, for the town is full of interest and the people are most friendly and hospitable.

We left with real regret and a longing to return.

The twisting Valley of the M'Zab, into which debouch many smaller valleys, is nearly thirty miles long, and in places impassable. To reach

GHARDAIA AT FLOOD TIME

Ghardaia from Guerrara it is therefore necessary to ascend once more to the bleak region of the Hamada and follow a track that winds over broken country in a south-westerly direction before striking the main valley again.

With a camel caravan the journey in normal conditions should take three days. Owing to unexpected bad weather we took seven, and were lucky to arrive at all.

Already delayed, we had planned to spend only two days at Ghardaia. But as a result of our experiences on the way, seven of the baggage camels went sick, and we had to wait for several days longer until fresh ones could be procured.

Yet, though we deplored the cause, we had reason to bless the further delay. Even had we been able to push on as soon as we expected, I very much doubt whether we could have torn ourselves away sooner from the fascinations or Ghardaia and her five sister towns.

Much had happened during the week since we left Guerrara. The long-overdue, much-prayed-for rain had come at last and in unusual abundance; the Oued M'Zab and the Oued N'Sa, together with many other smaller rivers, had rushed down in spate, and when we arrived Ghardaia was a city set on the banks of a lake— a sight seen only every ten years or so. The harvest, on which so much depends, assured, everyone was smiling and happy and the town was *en fête*. In all the *cafés maures* the tom-toms and pipes were banging and shrilling day and night, and the streets were thronged with rejoicing people. Even here was the ubiquitous gramophone. Strolling through the town after dark, when the merry-making was at its height, we passed shop after shop and café after café where attentive crowds sat listening with obvious delight to the raucous sounds projected from the gaily-painted horns—but the records were Arab music only, and the songs purely native ones sung by Arab singers.

At each town we visited, some bright lad or another would attach himself to us, for the length of our stay, to point out the places of interest and eagerly impart information.

At Ghardaia our self-appointed cicerone was a particularly intelligent little fellow of about ten years of age, not a Mozabite, but a Shambi, of whom there are a small number living in the town. The Shamba are a big tribe who spread out over a very large tract of country south of Ghardaia. Wild, lawless and utterly fearless, they are called the Lions of the Desert, and are very proud of themselves and their reputation. There is no love lost between them and the Mozabites, whom they despise for their peaceful, orderly ways.

To test our young friend we asked him if he was a Mozabite, and received an indignant denial.

" Then of what tribe are you ? " we asked.

THE MOZABITES

Up went the small head, and out went the small chest. " Shambi," he announced proudly.

" Oh, a Shambi," we teased. " But the Shamba are a very timid people who always run away when they are attacked."

"They are *not* a timid people," he snorted, "they are very brave, braver than all other people. And they do not run away. It is the Mozabites who run away."

" But here there are very many Mozabites, and very few Shamba," we reminded him. " What do you do when the Mozabite boys run after you ? "

" I beat them," came the swift reply. Then, swaggering deliciously : " I can beat two Mozabites, and *four Jews.*"

" But you shouldn't beat the Mozabites, they are very nice people," we said reprovingly.

" They are not nice people," he retorted, " and, also, they are not just. For, look you, when there is a disturbance in the town the Caid does nothing to the Mozabites. It is only the Shamba and the Jews who are sent to prison." Thus our young Daniel, and this too in the midst of a crowded street in the heart of the Mozabite capital. Certainly the Shamba are unafraid.

We went one evening to visit the principal Jewish synagogue, and found the chief Rabbi teaching a large class of boys, who were swaying backwards and forwards while they recited after him verses from the Book of the Law. They broke off their shrill sing-song for a moment or two when we entered, and the Rabbi, a venerable-looking old patriarch, greeted us courteously and sent a young priest to point out the few objects of interest. But unwilling to disturb further the class, we soon slipped away.

Very different from the Jewish school, where teachers and pupils all seemed like one happy family, and very different to the native schools with their keen and kindly young Kabyle masters, was the school of the White Fathers.

These White Fathers are a rich community, and at Ghardaia their establishment is a big one. Far too big it seemed for the needs of the few scholars who attend, and far too big to house the seven priests who live there. All large, well-nourished-looking men, with no trace of asceticism, all with the same fatal trait common to their kind—the inability to meet a frank glance frankly—they showed a cold, dispassionate and faintly hostile attitude that checked sympathy and was distinctly repellent.

Sharp-voiced and brusque in manner towards their pupils, they seemed to have no joy in their work, to be without the true inward love necessary to their calling, to be driven only by the dictates of stern duty.

In its way it was a tragedy, for behind it all one seemed to sense a bitter consciousness of failure.

The education they give is, I understand, sound, as far as it goes. But at Ghardaia the Fathers appear to concentrate more particularly on handicrafts, specializing in embroidery and leatherwork. Having first taught themselves, they ransacked Algeria for the different designs peculiar to the different tribes. And now some of the best work sold in the country comes from their workshops. But having learned his craft, the pupil leaves abruptly, and the White Fathers make no spiritual headway amongst their protégés.

The chapel is a large room of unusual shape. As I stood wondering at its unordinary proportions, I felt the Father's furtive eyes watching me. "It was not always a chapel?" I suggested. The Father shrugged his shoulders and smiled faintly.

"It was built for a hospital," he said rather sadly, "but these people, Madame, what will you? When they are sick they prefer their own doctors. And when they must die they prefer to die in their own homes."

Again failure, and a failure that left these big muscular men with nothing but women's work to do.

I thought of the progress that hospitals and dispensaries have made in India, and wondered whether it was the system or the administration that was at fault.

Adjoining the establishment of the White Fathers, and under the same management, is a community of White Sisters. But I did not feel drawn to investigate further the activities of the Order. One experience was enough, nor did the several White Sisters I saw moving about the town inspire me with any desire to become better acquainted with them. No doubt there are amongst the Order both men and women who are devoted and single-minded, but the mere layman is tempted to ask for what purpose is accumulated the wealth with which the Order is credited.

Within two miles of Ghardaia lie the fortified towns of M'lika, Benizguen, and Bounoura, each perched on a little hill, and each with its outer wall of defence rising from and welded into a basis of solid rock, so that in some places it is difficult to see where rock ends and masonry begins.

In M'lika we found an old potter, hard at work fashioning the handles for a dozen newly-made earthenware vessels. Half blind from the wood smoke of the bake oven in his hut, his fingers knarled and distorted with a lifelong handling of wet clay, he still worked, in spite of his age, with incredible speed, chuckling with pleasure as he rolled and finished one symmetrical piece of scroll work after another, proud of his craft, proud of his own skill.

They told him we were travellers, come from a far country to see the beauties of Algeria. His watery eyes twinkled and he beamed on us with a smile of sympathy and understanding—for was not he too a traveller? Algiers he knew, he asserted with a little quavering laugh. And once, yes, once he had gone across the big water even as far as Paris, where he had made pots and lamps for all the world to see in the Great Exhibition. And who in all the M'Zab had done as much? he added proudly. Few, we hastened to assure him. And few, we privately decided, would have returned to tiny distant M'lika as unspoiled as he from an experience that was evidently the outstanding achievement of his life.

Having time to spare, we rode one afternoon eight miles up the valley to El-Atteuf. Tucked away in a pocket at the foot of the hills, the little town seems to shrink timidly from sight, and there is no indication of its nearness until, rounding a tall shoulder of rock, one tumbles suddenly upon it. Smaller and less elaborately built than its sister towns, El-Atteuf has the appearance of being the poor relation of the family, and that day its bare, deserted streets helped to forward the impression. But it may be only an outward appearance. And its emptiness, we found later, was due to the fact that it was market day at Ghardaia and the whole of the male population of El-Atteuf had retired to the capital en masse.

Riding back in the cool of the evening, we were constantly meeting little companies of them returning home, strung out along the whole eight miles of the way, some on camels and some on mules, and all with pack-donkeys heavily laden. Shut in by tall red cliffs, its bareness broken here and there by clumps of dark green palm trees, the narrow winding valley was a place of beauty that tempted one to linger.

But this evening was our last in the M'Zab, our good-bye to the Mozabites, and we had to hurry back to Ghardaia to buy the last few necessaries before turning our faces towards the south.

IV

STORMBOUND

IT was in the wild mountainous country
between Guerrara and Ghardaia that our little
caravan nearly met with disaster.

The day we left Guerrara the weather showed
signs of change. The intense heat of the past few
days had given place to a raw, cold dampness, the
sky was grey overhead, while far away in the north
heavy black storm-clouds were piling up on the
horizon.

All day long they chased us, while we climbed
steadily up once more to the high plateaux, where
a piercing wind drove us hurriedly into extra coats
and burnouses.

Greyer and more than ever desolate appeared the
bleak Hamada, and it was difficult to believe that
only the day before we had been sweltering in
almost tropical heat.

With their shoulders hunched against the blast,
their heads muffled so that only half an eye was
visible, the men plodded doggedly on, the mules
and riding camels strung out one behind the other
making conversation impossible, for even a shouted

word was blown away and lost in the sharp gusts of wind. For hours we rode in silence, passing no other caravan and seeing nobody. Even the nomads avoid this bare stretch of sterile country.

Towards midday we dropped down again to a narrow boulder-strewn valley, and under lee of a tall cliff bordering a dried up river-bed we found a somewhat sheltered nook in which to lunch.

But though the overhanging rock broke the worst of the wind, it was not an ideal picnic spot, nor one in which to linger long. Yet here we had visitors, the first humans met since leaving Guerrara.

Our beasts first gave notice of their coming, the mules snorting and pawing uneasily, the camels flinging up their long necks to peer suspiciously up the valley. In the desert a camel, more especially a *mahari*, is as good as a watchdog. Overtaken by night, the traveller with a well-trained *mahari* will lie down beside his dumb companion and sleep peacefully, knowing that the *mahari* will not only give him timely warning of any approaching danger, but will also keep silent when it is remounted, should flight be necessary. It is only baggage camels, creatures of coarser clay, that roar and protest when they are being loaded.

Our visitors were two *goumiers*, searching for some stolen camels. Riding young half-broken *mahara*, they came padding swiftly down the dry river-bed, stopped to inquire if we had seen anything of the missing livestock, and finally stayed to

THE DRY BED OF THE OUED N'SA

share our servants' lunch. Slenderly built, wiry-looking men and, except for their accoutrements, differing little from the robbers they were pursuing, they were a cheery pair, who took in good part the jeers and badinage evoked by the antics of their untrained *mahara*, who, difficult to catch and baulky at starting, were not so eager as their masters to resume the long chase.

The wind dropped somewhat in the afternoon, which was fortunate for us. For that night we were forced to camp, having made only a bare eighteen kilometres during the day, on the top of a high plateau, where the tents had to be pitched in the open, without shelter.

Next morning we woke to find the same dreary grey sky and no improvement in the weather, while occasional cold splashes of rain gave promise of a coming deluge.

Again we worked down from the Hamada, striking at last a long, winding valley through which runs the Oued N'sa, or River of the Women. The bed of the river was still dry, but it was obvious that the long-delayed rain was not far off and the men were uneasy, for on the heels of the threatening storm would come the flood that pours down almost without warning.

Obliged to keep to the watercourse, for the steep banks were unclimbable, it was no place in which to be caught by a racing torrent, so we made what haste we could. But it was rough going, and big boulders and accumulated masses of débris left by previous inundations formed obstacles that hindered at every turn.

It was midday before the adjacent hills fell away suddenly and a sharp bend in the valley revealed more level ground and a break in the bank up which we scrambled, to halt for an hour or two at a *bordj* set some yards back from the verge of the river.

The guardians of these lonely rest-houses are usually shy, silent men, sometimes completely taciturn and uncommunicative. Their mode of life tends to make them so. Tied for years, and in many cases for all their years, to one spot, the dull monotony of their existence broken only by the occasional passing of a caravan, they lead lives of often grim isolation that must almost inevitably react on character and influence thought and speech. The companionship of wives and children keeps the married men human and sane, while the needs of a family—small though such needs may be—are an incentive to activity beyond the simple duties their guardianship entails. But there are others who, for one reason or another, elect to live absolutely alone. For these there is no incentive to work, no consideration of any kind beyond individual necessity. Small wonder they retire into themselves, and become dumb and morose. Yet there are some who rise above circumstance, whose spirits even stagnant isolation cannot quench. Such an one we found once, farther down in the south, in an ancient, half-ruined *bordj* built near an old, now

almost abandoned, caravan route. Though sometimes for months at a time seeing no human being,
this man was still neither silent nor gloomy.
Instead he was endowed with a light-hearted
gaiety that verged almost on the wild. Throughout
our stay he chatted unceasingly, breaking off into
peals of hilarious laughter, making the most of his
rare visitors. Perfectly contented with life he
appeared to be, his one distraction a few skinny
fowls whose eggs formed the major portion of his
meagre diet. In his isolation these eggs were
more valuable to him than money, and Kharbouch
had to exert his persuasive tongue to the utmost
to induce him to part with a few to add to our
fast-dwindling store.

Knowing the part that superstition plays in the
lives of the people, and the innumerable djinns and
afreets who are supposed to be ever present in
even the most humdrum localities, I asked my
men if he was not afraid to live in such a desolate,
haunted-looking spot, if no ghosts ever came to
trouble him in his loneliness.

" Ghosts, Madame ? " they laughed. " Why
should he be afraid of ghosts ? He is a ghost
himself ! " And, speaking of him afterwards, they
always referred to him as the Ghost.

Very different to the lot of the solitary Ghost
are the lives of the guardians of the *bordj* of the
Oued N'Sa. Here four brothers and their families
live together, their several tents pitched a few yards
away from the *bordj*, forming a tiny village which

is self-contained and self-supporting. Two of the brothers tend the rest-house, and keep in order a big storage tank—fed by the flood waters of the Oued N'Sa—which the Mozabites have built at this spot for times of drought, wells being scarce hereabouts and the route a recognized trade one. The two remaining brothers are employed as camel postmen between Guerrara and Ghardaia. One of these we were to see later, in circumstances we certainly never anticipated.

We ate our lunch in the *bordj*, to escape the cold drizzling rain that had set in, and waited another couple of hours for the arrival of the rest of the caravan, which that day had lagged far behind. For with the threatening weather and the chance of flood, we judged it wiser to remain altogether, rather than run the risk of being overtaken by the storm with the tents and camp equipment left miles in the rear and, perhaps, find them cut off from us entirely by the sudden flooding of one of the many rivers.

The rain held off again after lunch, and we went out to inspect the reservoir. Rectangular in shape, about 40 feet long and 10 feet broad, roofed in with a rounded top made of some cement-like material, and culminating at one end in a domed well-head, it looks like a gigantic tomb. No information could be obtained as to its depth, so it was impossible to gauge accurately its storage capacity. But, at a rough guess, it must be capable of holding, when full, about 20,000 gallons.

STORMBOUND

It was a strange thing to find lying out there in the desert, back of beyond. Instinctively one felt that there ought to be a power-house or some similar structure lurking somewhere in the vicinity. But, needless to say, there was nothing of the kind, nor, indeed, was there the simplest form of pumping apparatus to raise the stored water for use. The homely goat-skin, with a length of rope, did duty there as elsewhere.

The missing camels came in eventually, and we stayed to watch water-drums and goat-skins refilled, then pushed on for the afternoon stage, taking care to keep the remainder of the caravan well in sight.

The rain had stopped, but the outlook was far from encouraging, and we travelled on trying to find a spot where we might camp for the night in some degree of safety. The men, too, were not their usual cheery selves. For they knew now definitely that the storm was rolling up behind us, to break at any moment, and their constant backward glances became infectious, until at last I rode with my head slued perpetually over my shoulder, watching for the flood they seemed convinced would overtake us.

To have stayed at the *bordj*—even had it been advisable, which it was not, for the rooms are always several feet under water at flood time— would have meant the loss of valuable time and the subsequent probability of a lengthy detour, as we could never have crossed the swollen N'Sa.

We could only go on and trust to luck, hoping that the flood, if it came, would not be so large as our pessimists predicted.

A bitterly cold wind rose during the afternoon and continued to blow strongly, adding nothing at all to our comfort.

It was nearly dusk before we found, if not a suitable place, at least a place in which to camp. A tiny shallow ravine—remembered ever afterwards as the Ravin du Salut—set cup-wise between low hills, it was perhaps in the circumstances not the wisest choice of site, but we had no option. To have gone on in the darkness would have been madness.

There was very little merriment that evening, and a good deal of bickering and back-chat among the men, for they were rattled and working against time, pulling bales and boxes off the camels with more haste than care, rushing up tents, and tumbling over one another as they hauled on guy ropes and hammered in pegs.

A party went off to gather all the available brushwood in the neighbourhood for the kitchen fire, while the mules shrieked for their evening barley and C. and I tramped up and down trying to keep warm, longing for the delayed cup of tea, but tactfully avoiding the cook tent, from which came explosions of wrath as Kharbouch wrestled with damp sticks that would not burn, and fumed at a delay which, after all, was no fault of his. A devoted, orderly-minded soul, any departure from

OUR CAMP IN THE RAVIN DU SALUT

precedent was anathema to him. Accustomed, as were all my men, to shorter trips, farther in the north, where every inch of the ground is known to him, he preferred when starting in the morning to know definitely where the evening halt would be, that he might arrange to arrive first and have tents up and a kettle boiling when the rest of the party came in. But this was unknown country to him and to the others, a longer expedition than they had ever undertaken, where the usual order of things did not hold and where the unexpected was happening daily.

Scarcely were the tents up that first evening in the Ravin du Salut before the rain began again, but a soft, gentle rain that did not at all resemble the expected deluge.

We went to bed confident of an early start next morning. But alas, for our hope of reaching Ghardaia in scheduled time.

Early in the morning we awoke to the sound of a downpour, under which the tent was already slightly sagging, and a voice from without: " Impossible to march to-day."

At first we realized nothing but the unexpected luxury of a long lie, a late breakfast through which we should not have to scramble as usual, and the rare pleasure of a lazy day. So we drew up the blankets to sleep for another hour or two.

But as hour succeeded hour and the rain continued to fall steadily, the pleasure of a lazy day commenced to pall, and we began to wonder seriously how long we were to be held up by the weather, and what exactly we were in for.

Behind us lay the Oued M'Zab and the Oued N'Sa, before and all around stretched innumerable tributaries of the latter. Had the flood come? And, coming, would it spread to pour over and drown the adjacent country, our little ravine included?

Long before the evening we gave up asking questions. If it came, it came. And the knowledge of it was with Allah alone. There was nothing to be gained by speculation, nothing to do but wait.

These sudden floods are as great a menace in Algeria as they are in India. Countless damage is done and countless lives are lost in them. It was through the sudden flooding of the Oued Sefra that Isabelle Eberhardt—that strange stormy soul who lived for years in Algeria as an Arab among the Arabs—lost her life at Ain Sefra in October 1904, drowned in saving the life of her Arab husband, who could not swim.

It was a dreary day. We read a little, but books were few, for they take up valuable space and, camping, there is usually little time for reading. We repaired everything that needed repairing. Remained nothing—but to watch the rain, and wonder how long the tents would keep watertight.

Silence reigned throughout the camp. The camels were dispersed, but not very far away and with a couple of men rounding them up continually, while they cropped the scanty bushes that did not nearly fulfil their requirements.

Close by the mess tent the picketed mules stood shivering under their blankets, but gorging everything that came their way—they ate the straw coverings of the Evian bottles before we were done with the Ravin du Salut.

The men, personal servants and camel drivers alike, were hidden from sight inside the roomy cook tent. Occasionally a tentative thump on the tom-tom or a few plaintive notes from Lakada's flute came to our ears, but for the most part they slept, as only an Oriental can sleep—at any time and in any circumstances. Here, at last, the reason for taking that same big cook tent was justified. It had been a bone of contention from the first. Maama, the cameleer, whose camel had to carry it, had strenuously objected to it from the outset, swearing it was too heavy a burden for the darling of his heart, that it was unnecessary and would be unending trouble, and so on and so forth. Kharbouch, too, looked upon it with disfavour, since he infinitely preferred a smaller one, with which he had travelled for years, and to which he was accustomed. But wiser heads than theirs—and ours—had decreed otherwise, and after our experience in the Ravin du Salut we heard no more grumbling against the big cook tent.

Only Kharbouch remained awake, revising his

menus and preparing a colossal luncheon, which was followed in the evening by an equally colossal dinner.

Remonstrance was useless.

With his turban tipped over one ear, his dripping burnous adjusted at a nice angle, immaculate in spite of the mud, he stood over us while we ate—rather like a nurse with two refractory children—surveying us benignly, but firmly. " It is wet, it is cold," he announced severely, " and the ladies must eat, or they will be ill."

Privately we thought we were more in danger of being ill through over-feeding, but we had to submit, for our sensitive henchman would never admit lack of appetite and regarded an untasted dish as a slight to his cooking. That night, having plenty of time to prepare a meal, he served a *mesfouf*, a special kind of cous-cous cooked with raisins and eaten without a sauce, and a delicious chocolate *flan* made with fresh camel's milk.

All night the rain fell heavily, and next day it continued to pour down without ceasing, a regular deluge.

The wretched camels, unable to wander in search of food, lay in miserable wet heaps amongst the tents, gurgling and moaning, and snapping viciously at all who passed. The mules were huddled together shivering, tails to the wind, coughing under their saturated rugs and stamping uneasily on the ground which was slough under their feet.

The tents were standing up well and were still

watertight, but they were sagging considerably under the weight of moisture and we dared not touch the inside of the canvas lest a shower bath should descend.

We copied the men's good example and slept for most of the day. Towards evening one or two of the cameleers who had been out scouting brought back the rather disquieting news that the flood was sweeping the countryside and heading in our direction. There was, of course, the chance that it might split before reaching the camp and pass by on either side. On the other hand, it might just as readily pour through the little ravine and drown us all.

At the time I scoffed at the idea, and thought the men over-apprehensive. But I found out afterwards that during the last great flood, ten years ago, a party of five Arabs were caught by the racing torrent and drowned, together with their camels, not a quarter of a mile away from the Ravin du Salut.

In any case we could only wait, and hope for the best.

But whatever was to happen, some precautions had to be taken. Already the ground on which the camp was pitched had turned from a wet soggy mess into liquid mud, and it was slowly becoming a lake.

The heavy rain extinguished the acetylene flares as soon as they were lit, so by the solitary light of my electric torch the men worked for hours digging trenches round the tents and leading away from the camp, trying to drain off some of the water.

Their energy and devotion were wonderful. Wet through, their teeth chattering with cold, never once did they stop to think of their own discomfort. Their sole thought was that, at all hazards, C. and I must be kept as dry as possible.

With their white linen gandouras belted high above the knee, they flitted about in the darkness like pale spirits in some ghostly ballet. Indeed there was a curious feeling of unreality about it all. A feeling as though, sitting in a somewhat draughty box in a theatre, we were watching a very realistically staged performance of a Danse Macabre. There was an instinctive impulse to clap each time some slim, brown-legged figure halted for a moment in the broad beam of light issuing from the tent door—which beam made an excellent spot-light—to nod and smile cheerily.

Dinner that night was a fitful and protracted meal. Wrapped in woollen sweaters and great-coats, for it was bitterly cold, we sat with our heels curled up on our chairs, watching the water lapping into the entrance of the tent, now creeping steadily nearer, now receding as the men dug furiously. At long intervals Kharbouch would splash in with a disgusted grunt of "*Awā, awā*," and produce a dish from under his burnous, and then splash back to the cook tent to revive the sodden, shivering diggers with cups of boiling mint tea.

About ten o'clock there was a sharp thunderstorm, with vivid flashes of lightning.

By this time the camels were in a pitiable state, groaning miserably as they lay half submerged in deep pools of water, too wretched at last even to snap when we skipped past their recumbent forms in a quick rush to the sleeping tent.

We slept in our riding clothes, to be ready to run if the worst came to the worst—though goodness only knows where we could have run to.

In our damp cots we tucked in the blankets and, like Paul, prayed for the morning.

It was difficult to sleep. The camels, some of them lying close against the tent, kept up a continuous wailing, and several blundered up from time to time and thrust their silly heads through the fly, trying to force their way in to share our shelter; while every now and again some portion of our kit, piled precariously on rickety camp tables to be out of the wet, would fall with a thump on to the ground sheet, which meant a hasty dive into the cold to retrieve it.

We slept eventually, and slept so soundly that we never heard the commotion that occurred in camp just after midnight. It was not until the morning that we learned we had been the means of saving at least one man's life, and that man the camel postman between Guerrara and Ghardaia, one of the four brothers of the *bordj* by the Oued N'Sa.

Leaving Ghardaia on a swift *mahari* at dawn the previous day, he had struck the storm the first night out and, not daring to camp, had struggled on pluckily hour after hour until, frozen with cold and hunger and utterly bewildered with fear, he had lost all sense of direction. He had given himself up for lost and, numbed through, was on the point of slipping from his *mahari* to lie down and die, with the fatalistic passivity of his kind, when the *mahari* seems to have scented our camels and turned in the direction of the camp. He just saw the light shining out from the cook tent, where the men were all awake, and then collapsed. The poor fellow was in a terrible state when the men dragged him into the tent, and for hours they worked over him rubbing him with hot cloths and pouring boiling tea down his throat before he could even utter a word. But warmth and food and, above all, companionship, restored his morale; and, faithful to his mail-bags, he insisted on going on next day. We heard afterwards that he eventually reached Guerrara, but it must have been a bad trip, for he had to make a big detour to avoid the flooded N'Sa.

That day, our third in the ravine, there were a few odd moments when it did not rain, but by the afternoon it had settled down to a real soaker again.

Still, though food was running short and we had

begun to chaff Kharbouch and ask whether it was to be a mule or a camel that would be sacrificed first to satisfy the pangs of hunger, we were all very cheerful. For we knew now that the flood had providentially passed on either side of the little ravine, and we were not to be drowned like rats in a hole.

Bread was one of the first things to give out, but there was still some flour, so we ate instead the Arab substitute—flat dough cakes, rather like Indian *chapattis*. Firewood, too, was becoming a difficulty, for the brushwood the men brought in was too saturated to do more than fill the cook tent with volumes of smoke that set everybody weeping and coughing. Fortunately by this time there were some empty packing-cases which helped to keep the fire burning.

In the desert this problem of firewood is often an acute one, second only to water, for sometimes, when most needed, it is impossible to find, and there are not always packing-cases available. There was an occasion once—but that is a dark history, relating to some spare telegraph poles belonging to the French Government, that must not be enlarged upon. Only let the excuse be that the need was great.

No longer in danger of drowning, and with the young camels to fall back on if it came to a pinch, the only care now was how soon would the weather clear sufficiently to allow of the soaked tents being packed and a fresh start made.

CAMPING IN THE SAHARA

Badly in need of exercise, we managed a short walk in the morning, but the ground was a quagmire that soon drove us back to the tents.

Fine rain set in again during the afternoon, and the possibility of a start seemed further off than ever.

All that night it rained, gently but persistently, and we slept with our heads under the blankets, for cold splashes of water were at last dripping from the over-weighted canvas.

Next morning, however, there were shouts of joy, for not only had the rain stopped, but a high wind was blowing that was calculated to dry the tents enough, at least, to pack.

All the morning anxious eyes watched the weather, while half a gale roared through the ravine, making the tents flap like mad things. But the wind was a god-send, and we whistled for more, for it was doing its work well.

The sky, that for the last four days had been a dull uniform grey, was broken up into a mass of hurrying, tumbled clouds, and away to windward a bright streak spread across the horizon.

Midday came, then a hurried packing up at express speed—with blankets and burnouses flying in all directions, and the men dancing like maniacs on the tents to get them flat enough to roll—a last good-bye to the Ravin du Salut, and we were off.

But twelve kilometres was all that could be accomplished that afternoon. The going was

A WELL IN THE DESERT

awful. The track, which from here on to Ghardaia is usually fairly distinct, was in most places completely obliterated. There were big cavities and wash-outs to be avoided, and the ground was giving way continually under the beasts' feet. They did their best, poor things, but they were stiff and chilled through from the exposure of the last few days. The camels particularly were in a bad way, and there were grave doubts whether some of them would last even as far as Ghardaia. So haste was out of the question.

That night we had to camp on the top of a high plateau, with the gale still shrieking, and the men spent most of the night hanging on to the tents, that threatened every moment to blow away. It was one of the coldest nights I have ever experienced. The sky was uniformly grey again next morning, and the wind blowing cold and strong as ever. It was pitiful to watch the sick camels struggling under their loads, but the only chance of saving them was to get them into Ghardaia as soon as possible, so we had to harden our hearts and push on.

The last stage into Ghardaia was a punishing one. And wilder and even more desolate than the approach to Guerrara became the scenery as we neared the capital of the M'Zab. Stark rock and arid bareness stretched on either side, a tumbled, tortured tract of country, probably volcanic in origin, that looked as if it had been torn up and flung down again haphazard by some angry giant in wanton play.

All day long we toiled over rugged hills and valleys, through steep defiles where the beasts slithered and slipped trying to keep a precarious foothold.

But these steep defiles, difficult though they were, were only a slight preparation for the two final descents that were to bring us once more to the level of the M'Zab Valley.

Mounting steadily upward between hills which, grown taller and more bold in outline, now showed ancient stone-built watch-towers crowning their heights, we came to the end of a long, winding pass, and saw before us what appeared to be a sheer precipice, while hundreds of feet below lay the Valley with its four closely-grouped towns.

It was a scene of wild and almost unparalleled grandeur, from which we turned reluctantly to the problem that confronted us. The descent seemed impossible, even for the mules, let alone the ailing camels. It was a moment when we longed for an aeroplane. This picturesque but tremendous entrance to Ghardaia is not the ordinary caravan route. For trade caravans the descent is too steep and too dangerous, and the recognized trail makes a wide-sweeping detour round the higher hills and enters the Valley by a less precipitous path. We had branched from the longer though safer track early in the morning, partly for the sake of the magnificent view, partly for the sake of the beasts. For, for them, the bad descent was preferable to another night spent in the open, without food, when some of the camels might have lain down to rise no more.

A sour-tempered beast, perhaps the most sour-tempered of all, the camel has yet one redeeming quality—faithfulness to duty. With a pack on his back he will struggle against almost overwhelming odds to reach his journey's end, often to die as soon as his load is lifted. And for this saving grace much can be forgiven him.

The longer we looked at that fearsome descent the less pleasant it became. But a way down there was, and we reached the bottom intact— only to find ourselves on a wide terrace of flat stone, that hung sheer above the Valley, with another hitherto hidden but now painfully apparent descent, far worse than the first, yawning at our feet.

Not even our wonderful mules, surefooted as cats, could carry us down that second gully. And how any of the animals reached the level without broken legs and backs is a still abiding wonder.

The caravan went on first and, waiting at the head of the ravine, looking out over the marvellous view, I tried to keep myself from doing sums, from calculating what the descent was going to cost in camel-flesh. The poor beasts' piteous cries of terror made one feel sick.

It seemed hours before they all got down, and down, mercifully, without any accident.

CAMPING IN THE SAHARA

What they had been through we saw for ourselves when our own turn came.

It was a risk that would never have been taken had the real nature of the ground been known beforehand.

Ghardaia was reached without the loss of a single camel. But the seven sick ones were so badly knocked up after their experience in the Ravin du Salut that we had to leave them in the M'Zab, where they eventually recovered, and get fresh ones to go on with us down into the south. In this way we lost little Angelica, whose mother was among the invalids. But Diavolo remained, to be a constant joy to the end of the trip.

V

BANDITS

AFTER leaving the M'Zab Valley we had planned to avoid the recognized caravan trade routes and travel straight across the mountains due south to El-Goléa.

But at Ghardaia we learned that the stretch of country we proposed to cross, which is part of the territory of the Shamba tribe, was swarming with bandits, and that to attempt to get through without a guard of *goumiers*—Arab soldiers—would be impossible. Bandits are common in many districts of Algeria, so the information was not unexpected. But there are often ways of overcoming the seemingly impossible and, bandits or no bandits, I was determined to go on, and equally determined, for many reasons, to take no *goumiers* with me. To travel with a military escort of any kind was quite outside my prearranged scheme. Not only would their presence have hampered my movements, but I should have been received everywhere with suspicion instead of the open confidence I desired, and I should not have seen and heard the things I wished to see and hear. Nor did I want by any show of distrust to forfeit the title of "Friend of the Arabs" which I had been fortunate enough to gain.

Also, I had more confidence in my own men than in any escort that might be allotted to me. They were loyal and devoted, and their personal courage we had already had occasion to test fairly early in the trip.

Though they may be speaking in all sincerity, it is not always wise when travelling in Algeria to take as gospel the assurances of either the military authorities or local chiefs that the country is peaceful and quiet. Leaving on one side any question of sporadic risings, which still continue despite all contradictory statements supplied to the Press, inter-tribal quarrels are perpetually occurring and sometimes rage for weeks without the knowledge of the Government.

At Hadjïera the Caid had confidently affirmed, and he spoke in perfect good faith, that there was no disturbance in the neighbouring district. Yet within a short time of leaving his jurisdiction, while passing from the territory of the Ouled Sayeh to that of the Ouled Naïl, we found that serious trouble had broken out between these two tribes, and when we came on the scene they were shooting at sight.

Our way lay between the disputing parties.

It was an anxious few days, during which a double guard was kept round the tents each night, for two of our own men belonged to the Ouled Sayeh, and it was just a question whether the Ouled

Nail—a treacherous and crabbed-minded people—
might not make that a pretext for attacking us,
coupled with the fact that, at the moment, anyone
who crossed their path was, in their opinion, fair
game.

But though we sighted several scouting
parties, and even spoke with some—after their
women had been first sent to reconnoitre—we got
through unmolested. And, happily ended, the
little *contretemps* merely remained an incident we
were glad to have experienced, for it proved the
mettle of our men, who all behaved admirably.
Even Karbouch the timorous sat up valiantly o'
nights with the inevitable cigarette dangling in
one hand and a big revolver clutched in the
other.

These inter-tribal disputes nearly always result
from one of two causes—camels and women, and
I put them in the relative order in which they
are usually regarded. In this case it was a camel,
by Arab standard the more valuable animal. A
man of the Ouled Nail had stolen a camel belonging to a tribesman of the Ouled Sayeh. The
owner started in hot pursuit, and finding no trace
of the thief or his missing property, promptly shot
the thief's brother as nearest of kin, that being
the proper and correct mode of retaliation. It
then became a blood feud in which both tribes
joined with characteristic eagerness.

But though I had proved my men, a few days'
quick rush through disputing tribes was a very

different proposition to weeks of travelling over difficult country with always the constant menace of attack.

It was too much to expect of them, besides which I knew that our own force was too small to get the caravan through safely should the bandits be as numerous and as attentive as they were reported. In a still somewhat lawless country the general tendency is usually to cry " Wolf." But discreet inquiries, made the first night at Ghardaia, established the fact that, this time, the popular bogey was not being raised for our benefit, and it was unanimously agreed that if we persisted in going on there would have to be an escort of some kind. The question only remained, Who ? At first the problem seemed insoluble. In the end it was arranged quite simply, though in a novel fashion I never anticipated.

That we were able to carry out our programme and travel not only safely, but in absolute security through the bandit region was due entirely to Si Aly Sab. An Arab himself, and known by repute through Algeria for his political activities, he had ways of approaching and dealing with his own people that were not for the mere traveller.

In the course of his inquiries word came to him in some circuitous manner that our best plan was to send a message to the chief of the bandits, explaining who and what we were and asking for a safe conduct through his country. I must own that the *naïveté* of the suggestion appealed to me, so, to cut a long story short, the message was sent. In a few days the answer came that the bandit chief himself would be happy to convoy the English ladies and take them where they wished to go.

Truly Algeria is the land of the unexpected, and the more one travels there the less one comes to feel surprise at anything.

Just what were the arguments put forward to induce this shy gentleman to lend us his protection I never sought to learn. It was enough that the way was made easy, without bothering as to the whys and wherefores.

Since it was impossible for our redoubtable escort to join us in the capital of the M'Zab, by reason of former exploits which have won for him, among other more or less picturesque sobriquets, the title of the " Terror of Ghardaia," our meeting was arranged to take place near the village of Metlili.

For the two days' journey to Metlili we took on some Shamba to guide us through the mountains, and with these, together with a small caravan that was travelling for a short distance in our direction and which joined itself to us for protection, we made quite a large party.

A long, stiff climb took us out of the Valley of the M'Zab and brought us into wild, mountainous country that was more grandly beautiful than anything we had yet seen. And the two steep approaches to Ghardaia paled to insignificance before the formidable gorges and defiles up and down which we slithered and scrambled on that day and many succeeding days. Often the way was so narrow that there was only room to ride single file, through deep shadowy cañons that curved and twisted confusingly, past tall cliff faces where great masses of protruding rock seemed threatening every moment to fall on our heads, and over ground so broken up and weathered that we could only move at a snail's pace.

Small wonder bandits exist in a land so ideally formed by nature for guerilla warfare of any kind; in some of the defiles through which we toiled ten men could have held up a regiment, while an army could have lain concealed amongst the tortuous windings of the hills and been passed unseen. The fate of a caravan caught in one of these narrow passes by the predatory inhabitants must be sudden and swift. Prompt and abject surrender may occasionally leave them with just their lives, though stripped of camels and merchandise and even the food with which to prolong life. Any show of resistance results in complete and thorough extermination—which, after all, is perhaps kinder in the long run, for a quick death by a bullet is easier than a slow one from starvation.

Ever since we entered the bandit country I had marked and been intrigued by numerous little heaps of stones set at odd intervals beside the

OUR CARAVAN ON THE MARCH THROUGH THE BANDIT COUNTRY

track. They were like, and yet not altogether like, the stone cairns built ordinarily to distinguish a caravan route. But here we were off any recognized caravan route and, looking at them, I wondered. Eventually I guessed, but asked to make sure. And they were, as I thought, the graves of those who had fallen victim to bandits. At one place we saw a group of fifteen or sixteen set close together, and learned that it marked the spot where an entire bridal party had been wiped out.

It was a cheery little reminder of the hazards of life, but we knew that our coming was watched for, and we were able to view the sinister little graves with an equanimity we should otherwise not have felt.

Hyenas are said to abound in this neighbourhood, but though the Shamba guides pointed out many dens amongst the rocks, we neither saw nor heard them. Jackals are few; there are no large packs here as in the Aurès Mountains, and the few, happily, were not vocal.

Neither panther nor wild boar are found so far south, and the only hunting cries heard at night were those of owls and a small kind of wild cat.

We struggled all day through these labyrinthine hills, scrambling up precipices to slide down the other side and begin all over again. They seemed never ending and the camels made very heavy weather over the rough ground, lagging behind at every opportunity. At noon we halted in a ravine; when night came we slept in a ravine.

With true desert independence, or suspicion, the Shamba made their camp and built their fire some little distance from our men; while, further away again, the traders—who were gone before daybreak next day—lit yet a third fire to cook their evening cous-cous. It was here that we had a little example of family rule as practised amongst the Arabs, where the younger members of a family are, theoretically, completely subject to their elders.

The principal Shamba guide was an old man with rigid and old-fashioned ideas, particularly with regard to smoking, which, though it is forbidden by the Koran, is nowadays almost universally practised throughout the country. This man had with him a nephew, a stalwart rather truculent-looking young fellow of certainly five or six and twenty, whose own ideas were very much more up to date and liberal. Helping our men to make camp that evening he had succumbed to a longing for the forbidden thing, and begged a cigarette from Kharbouch. But his courage did not carry him the length of flaunting his treasure under his austere uncle's nose, and later, when strolling in the twilight, we found him hidden in a big *drinn* bush, puffing surreptitiously and looking, when he saw us, for all the world like a naughty schoolboy caught smoking under a hedge. But we played the game and never told uncle.

BANDITS

Metlili is built on the side of a hill, with a broad river flowing at its base, and overlooking a fertile little oasis-like valley which is filled with palm trees and vegetable gardens.

Through a narrow defile, passing between tall, overhanging cliffs, one rounds a sharp spur of rock and comes upon the village suddenly. One of its most outstanding features is the cemetery, situated on the opposite hillside. Hewn out of the living rock, and filled in with heavy stones, the graves are placed very close together, and rise one above the other on a series of natural terraces, with here and there a built-up masonry platform to support the whitewashed tomb of some sheik or other person of distinction.

Our own bandit—as we had come to think of him—who is, incidentally, a chief of high standing, ruling over a big district, was waiting for us a day's journey beyond Metlili. But we stopped for an hour at the village to drink tea with some of his relations and to buy eggs and chickens. This last was a lengthy business, for eggs came in slowly and one by one, the shy toddlers who brought them having to run home again half a dozen times before mother would accept the sum offered; while the local price of feathered fowl was such that Kharbouch metaphorically rolled up his shirt sleeves and sat down to a prolonged and vituperative bargaining. So we left him to it and went to explore the little town.

In the old days, before the advent of modern

artillery, Metlili, like the Mozabite towns, must have been impregnable. Even now it looks capable of withstanding a siege, so cleverly are rock and masonry intermingled.

In the heart of the town is a little mosque built curiously round the four sides of a colonnaded courtyard where, in times of war, the women and children were placed for safety.

The people, unused to visitors, were shy of showing themselves ; half-open doors were gently pushed to at our approach, but excited whispering could be heard inside, and a quick glance backward always showed a row of furtive peeping heads. Those we met were courteous, though uncommunicative. Nor were the family with whom we went to drink mint tea any more voluble, but our visit obviously gave pleasure, and I am certain the secluded ladies heard all about it afterwards, down to the very last detail of our personal appearance.

When we came to start again it was easy to see from Kharbouch's self-satisfied swagger who had had the best of the bargaining. And though he professed contempt for the eggs, which were small, he was pleased to approve of the sixteen frenzied fowls who were squawking dismally on the back of one of the baggage camels.

From the comparatively low level of Metlili we climbed again to the top of a high plateau, the summit of which was formed of enormous slabs of marble-like rock that looked like giant paving-

METLILI, THE BANDIT STRONGHOLD

stones. As some of the slabs were set at rather an acute angle, down which the mules tobogganed gleefully and the camels protestingly, our attention was focussed on the Crestas we were negotiating, and we found little leisure in which to admire the magnificent view.

From there we dropped down, about 1500 feet, by a tremendously long and steep descent to the broad valley of the Oued Seb-Seb. Here we camped for the night, and had our first and last disagreement with the new camel men we had taken on at Ghardaia. They had shown a growing discontent at what they termed our too rapid mode of travelling, and that evening at Seb-Seb their discontent found utterance. But they were tactfully and firmly dealt with by Si A. S. and gave no more trouble for the rest of the time they were with us. Though it was an annoying incident, there was an element of humour in it, for during the necessary sermon preached at the malcontents our own camel men and our personal servants wore such smug faces of superiority and self-righteousness that it was difficult to keep from laughing.

Next day our famous bandit joined us. With no escort or display of any kind he came in quite quietly with only one man, his trusted lieutenant, accompanying him. Just what we had expected I don't quite know, but the reality was altogether different to anything we had imagined. Gentle-mannered and low-voiced, he greeted us with simple dignity that was charming. And, listening to his soft utterances, it was hard to believe that this shy, friendly little man was really the perpetrator of the deeds of violence and bloodshed with which, particularly in his youth, his name is associated. Latterly, I understand, he has rather withdrawn from active participation in the outrages conducted by his tribesmen. But he still occasionally takes the field, and he has the reputation of being a kind of Arab Robin Hood, for, with a nice discrimination, he now almost entirely confines his attention to the rich, whom he robs to give to the poor.

His kind, rather benevolent face does not suggest either the relentless bandit or the arbitrary despot. It was only later, when travelling through his territory, that we realized somewhat of his far-reaching influence and gathered, from the servile attitude of several of the very rich nomads, some idea of the extent of his authority. And later still, when I returned to the north, I had full confirmation of his reputation and was amused to see the interest and excitement amongst certain of the Arabs when they learned who had been my escort.

With us he was always mildness itself, and we became great friends.

For a month he convoyed us, to El-Goléa in the south and then back across the nomad country as far as Ouargla, where he left us hastily, before his identity became known, for personal and delicate reasons connected with his achievements.

It was because of his abrupt departure that we have, unfortunately, no photograph of him or his lieutenant. For having purposely delayed snapping him until he should leave us, and not expecting him to make such a sudden exit, the moment of his going found the camera empty, and he did not care to risk waiting even while we delved amongst our kit for a fresh roll of films. We parted with mutual regret, and assurances on his part that he would travel with us any time and anywhere we wanted, even though it might be to the Hoggar Mountains or Timbuctoo !

After the coming of our bandit—whose name I prefer not to disclose—we were able to revert to our usual practice of leaving the slow-moving baggage camels, with the cameleers, to make their own way during the day, and rejoining them only in the evening. For with the chief to look after us, and his lieutenant to safeguard the caravan with our belongings, there was no longer any need to keep together for safety's sake, and we were again able to go our own pace and make detours when any special attraction presented itself.

At the same time, we paid off the Shamba who had guided us thus far from Ghardaia.

So in the care of this formidable little man we journeyed through a dangerous zone in perfect security, sleeping peacefully in our beds at nights, hob-nobbing on occasions with bands of sinister-looking cut-throats whose appearance we should not otherwise have enjoyed, and without experiencing adventures that might have made this a much more entertaining narrative—had we survived to write it.

As it was, for ourselves, the nature of the country we were traversing provided full and ample excitement. Had I not seen it myself, I should not have believed it possible for camels to negotiate the tremendous climbs and really terrifying descents which we encountered on our way through that wild mountainous district. Providence was undoubtedly kind, but it was also due to the constant watchfulness and care of the men that not only we, but all the animals also got through without broken bones or any serious injury. In fact the only bad accident that occurred during the trip was in no way owing to the nature of the ground, but was the result of pure carelessness coupled with conceit. It happened when we were nearing Ouargla, weeks after we had left the mountains. Starting early one morning with the firm intention of making a record march, for we had lost time and gone five days out of our way hunting for a well, as we were badly in need of water, we had ridden for seven hours without a stop through a district that was filled with immense Chotts, salt depressions or lakes, which at that season were dry. These Chotts are most unpleasant to cross, and often there is no means of avoiding them, for the glare of the sun on the salt is blinding, while the atmosphere is so impregnated with it that one's lips crack and bleed. We had just crossed a Chott of eight miles in length when the irrepressible Lakada, always bubbling over with high spirits, announced that he was going to ride one of the *maharis*, whose master was at the moment walking. The *mahari* was a particularly vicious, nasty-tempered beast, and Lakada was not an experienced rider, though he thought himself equal to the best. We all shouted to him to be careful, but, scornful of warnings, he grabbed a heavy whip and leaping on to the *mahari* started off at full gallop. If he had left it at that, all might have been well. But a mere gallop was too tame a proceeding for our cheerful mountebank. Endeavouring to impress us with his skill, he tried to make the animal show off its paces, with the result that it swerved suddenly and then stopped dead. We saw Lakada shoot out of the saddle, describe a graceful parabola through the air, and fall with a crash on his head. In dismay we raced up to him, expecting to find him with at least a dislocated neck. Happily no bones were broken, but he was in a very bad way, suffering from concussion and with the muscles of his head and neck severely wrenched. We had to make camp there and then on the edge of the Chott, and do what we could for him with the few appliances we had to hand. For a day or two we thought he would die, but he recovered slowly, though he was on the sick-list and unable to walk or do anything for the remainder of the journey.

It was six days after the coming of our bandit before we got clear of the main range of mountains. On the high plateau the wind was still very strong and cold, so cold that sometimes, with hands and feet completely numbed, it was impossible to ride, and we had to walk for hours to restore circulation.

Leaving the mountains at last, we entered once more into a sandy region, where only low hills hemmed in a succession of long, wide valleys.

The change to soft ground and easy going was a welcome relief, particularly for the camels, whose feet were beginning to show signs of wear from the hard rock. Down in the valleys the change of temperature was very noticeable, and from now onwards we travelled in almost tropical heat.

But before leaving the mountains we were joined by a little party of three, quite the most interesting of all those who, at various stages, attached themselves to us for longer or shorter periods during the trip. This delightful trio consisted of a *maharist*, belonging to the Saharan Camel Corps, who after three months' leave of absence in the north was returning with his children, a boy and a girl, to rejoin his corps at Timimoun. The *maharist* was a fine type of Arab, smart and soldierly looking, deferential in manner, though without the least tinge of servility, and devoted to his children. The boy, a round-faced sturdy lad of twelve, was soon a great favourite amongst the men, and made himself very useful in camp; while the girl, a shy, pretty little thing, wonderfully dressed and obviously the apple of her father's eye, quickly became the pet of the whole caravan. From the first their homeward journey had been a series of disasters. Starting out on camelback—for every *maharist* going on leave has to take with him his own corps *mahari*—the camel had died as the result of an accident. This meant not only loss of time, but also a big pecuniary loss as well, for the animal being Government property, the *maharist* would have himself to refund its cost when he rejoined at Timimoun.

Afraid of overstepping his leave, he bought a horse, but ill-luck dogged him and the horse died also. By this time, unable to afford anything better, in desperation he bought a donkey—and a few nights later the wretched little beast slipped its hobbles and ran away. So the family were reduced to tramping, except the small girl, who was carried in her father's arms. To cap everything they were caught, and nearly died from exposure, in the same storm that delayed us in the Ravin du Salut. Fortunately they were found and brought into Ghardaia a few days after our own arrival there.

Hearing that we were bound for the south, under protection, they hastened to overtake us and ask for assistance and escort as far as El-

Goléa, where they hoped to find some caravan that would take them on down to Timimoun, which they eventually did. But by the time we reached El-Goléa the poor *maharist's* leave was expired, and he begged Si Aly Sab to write a letter to his Commandant explaining what we knew of the case, which letter I hope served him in good stead, for it corroborated another he had had the forethought to procure from the authorities in Ghardaia.

During the day father and son walked with the men. But a soft nest was made for the little girl on top of one of the baggage camels, where she rode happily, looking, in her bright clothing, like some gay tropical bird. At night they made their camp close to ours, just a windbreak of blankets and burnouses, but, with a brushwood fire to warm them, it was cosy and comfortable and all they were accustomed to.

We used to pay a call every evening on little Miss Maharist to inquire for her health and ask how she had stood the fatigues of the day. But it was proud papa who did all the talking, for she was much too shy to do more than smile and peep at us furtively. But she learned to look for us each morning when we started out, and to respond to our hand-wavings with a tentative flourish of her tiny henna-stained fingers.

After leaving the mountains the weather changed completely. There was no more rain, and the dull grey storm clouds gave place to a clear blue sky out of which the sun beat down fiercely. Even the nights were hot; but they were nights of enchantment, with the countless great stars blazing in the heavens, with the deep solemn silence that is one of the desert's greatest wonders, with the faint sweet smell of a million tiny flowers, which, born in a night to bloom for a few brief fragrant hours, carpet the sand sometimes for miles at a time with sheets of mauve and yellow.

Nearing El-Goléa, we wondered if we would be fortunate enough to meet any of those far-famed black-veiled raiders of the south, the Touareg of the Hoggar Mountains. They come up periodically as far as El-Goléa, where leather-work made by their women can be bought. But though we looked for them hopefully, we saw only a solitary Targui, an ancient man who boldly proclaimed his nationality, but who, with his black veil laid aside, might as easily have passed for a Shambi.

The most picturesque-looking bandit with whom we became acquainted we picked up in a nomad's camp after leaving El-Goléa. Supposed to know the whereabouts of a well for which we were hunting, he travelled with us for five days, a hardened old reprobate of over seventy who gloried in his inglorious career, and only regretted that age and the lack of a modern weapon prevented him from assuming his former activities.

Ibraheim ben Chem ben Boukhachba, commonly

called " The Man of Forty-five Murders "—for that
was the least number he would admit to—has
been a bandit all his days, with a reputation for
ferocious cruelty. He was also deeply implicated
in the rebellion of the Sheik Bou Amama against
the French, which lasted from 1900 to 1902. The
rising finally suppressed, the two men fled together
to Morocco, where Bou Amama died, and Ibraheim remained in hiding until two years ago, when
he was pardoned by the French Government and
allowed to return to Algeria. Now he roams
about, always alone, from nomad's camp to nomad's camp, living on his past reputation, getting
without payment everything for which he asks,
staying here a day and there a week as the fancy
takes him, and sighing for the good old days
that will never come again.

Suspicious of us and taciturn at first, the night
he joined us he made his lonely little camp at
some distance, praying at sunset with a fervid
and ostentatious show of piety the hypocrisy of
which probably never occurred to him, though it
occasioned much mirth among the men who had
learned something of his history from the nomads.
The second night he came a little nearer. The
third night nearer still, and after supper he strolled
over and talked for a little while with the camel
drivers. But the fourth night, encouraged, no
doubt, by their curiosity, he grew communicative,
and the whole camp sat up until daybreak listening
open-mouthed like children, with rapt and eager

"THE MAN OF FORTY-FIVE MURDERS"

attention, to his horrible tales of violence and bloodshed, for which he showed no remorse, no repentance, nothing—but a savage pride in his achievements and regret that life was now so tame.

They told me afterwards that during some of his stories he seemed to be living the whole scene over again, and worked himself up to such a pitch of emotion that the sweat poured down his face and his whole body trembled with excitement. His ancient six-foot-long flintlock, the barrel of which was lapped round with copper wire that undoubtedly belonged to the Telegraph Department of the French Army, was a fearsome and wonderful relic I would like to have bought, not only as a genuine antique, but as an example of what a gun will come through and yet function. But he was proud of his alarming weapon, which must be much more dangerous to the shooter than the shot at, and, his living provided free wherever he goes, money was no temptation to him.

That the hoary old ruffian knew we had been made acquainted with the full details of his discreditable history was evident the morning he left us, for his swagger was superb and his blatant self-satisfaction almost laughable. But the height of his vanity was reached when C. snapped him, and though he had never before in his life seen a camera, he posed with all the nonchalance and assurance of an established film favourite.

Last, but not least, among the bandits of our

acquaintance must be included a man who travelled with us, as a trusted personal servant, not only throughout the length of this trip, but during another journey taken two years ago. He, rather than the bandit chief, deserves the name of our very own bandit. Very early in his career he became an outlaw and acquired fairly extensive fame. But he fell into the hands of the authorities at last, and when he first travelled with us he had just been released from serving two years' imprisonment. It was due to the kindness of heart of the late Messaoud ben Akli, who was always helping lame dogs over stiles, that he was given a chance to reform and make a new start in life. It was taking chances, but the experiment proved a brilliant success. And the ex-bandit became a devoted and absolutely trustworthy servant, who would have gone through fire and water for his patron. So assured was I of his sincerity and attachment that I specially included his name in the list of men I wanted to accompany me on this last trip into the wilds. And should I ever be in a tight corner anywhere in the Sahara, I should like to have that cheery, reliable little ex-bandit with me.

By us his former calling was always tactfully ignored, nor was he, on his first journey with us, inclined himself to be communicative on the subject, even with his fellow servants. But time eventually served to loosen his tongue, and one day during this last journey, while we were still in the north, memories connected with the locality through which we were passing seemed to break down his reserve, and he burst into a flood of reminiscence.

Arabs are interminable talkers, and their incessant conversation between themselves often leaves one wondering what they can find to talk about. But that day I wondered more than ever what could be the engrossing topic on which the little man was holding forth so eloquently and with such a wealth of dramatic gesture, and which was so completely absorbing the attention of Kharbouch—beside whose camel he was walking —who, for once dumb himself, was stooping low in the saddle lest one word should escape him, and throwing himself back from time to time with peals of laughter that threatened to make him lose his usually more or less precarious seat.

It transpired that our lighthearted ex-bandit was entertaining his more staid companion with accounts of his former doings, pointing out various spots where he had held up caravans, and explaining his methods of dealing with his victims. Shorn of the necessary brutality, it seems to have been a humorous recital, that doubtless lost nothing in the telling, for Kharbouch giggled periodically for days afterwards and kept on making pointed allusions which his now somewhat abashed informant pretended not to hear, but which convulsed the other men.

And that he still remains an abiding memory

with some people, was shown at a village outside
of which we camped, where a decidedly forward
young woman, coming to sell eggs and remaining
to flirt with "the Sentimentalist," having caught
one glimpse of our notorious henchman, uttered a
wild shriek and fled to return no more. Whether
she thought we were all bandits together, I do not
know, but it certainly looked like a case of *ex uno
disce omnes.*

VI

THE GARDEN IN THE WILDERNESS

EACH day as we drew nearer to El-Goléa the sun beat down more fiercely, while a persistent sirocco filled the air with tiny particles of sand that drifted through into everything and stung like splinters of glass.

From a region of high sand dunes we passed gradually to long rolling stretches of undulating country, which in turn gave place to a succession of big, basin-like valleys shut in by curious, conical-shaped hills split up by innumerable ravines.

Though not true nomads, the Shamba, in whose territory we still were, are nomads at heart. Preferring life in the open, they leave their villages and gardens for the greater part of the year in the charge of a few old men and women and migrate by families into the desert, where they live in tents, moving from place to place to supply the needs of their flocks and herds.

In the breeding season their camel mares congregate in these basin-like valleys and on the warm slopes of the sand-dunes to give birth to their young, usually a single foal, though twins are not uncommon. Almost from the first the foals are hardy, independent little things, who quickly learn to take care of themselves—a wise provision of nature, for with camels the maternal instinct is rather dormant than active. Beyond supplying the necessary nourishment in a somewhat grudging and peevish manner, they seem to take little interest in their offspring, and rarely exhibit alarm, let alone anger, when one stops to look at or even handle them.

We saw many such families, the supercilious-eyed mothers grazing haughtily apart, the youngsters gambolling grotesquely as they played a kind of King of the Castle up and down the sandy hillocks.

Some of the foals were only just born. Too weak still to stand, they sprawled on the warm sand, ungainly little woolly bundles that looked all legs and neck, bleating feebly and making futile efforts to get on to their feet.

Being a valuable asset, they are usually well treated by their owners, and though they start when very young to run with their mothers in the caravans, they are rarely worked before they are two years old.

The special breeds bred by the different tribes are commonly distinguished by their colour, which ranges from black through all shades of brown down to pale yellow and finally pure white, so it is easy to tell at a glance to what tribe any particular camel belongs. But since they are frequently sold from one part of the country into another, every camel is also branded with the distinctive mark of the owner's tribe.

The pure white camels are peculiar to the Touareg. With very slender, delicately-shaped limbs and small, intelligent-looking heads, they are really beautiful creatures, and famous for their speed. Seen against a background of deep golden sand they appear almost dazzlingly white, and, with their clean-cut limbs and graceful movements, are easily the aristocrats of the camel world. They are all *mahara*, and are consequently not used in caravans. Altogether they differ from the ordinary camel as much as does a racehorse from a Clydesdale.

The nomadic instinct is not confined exclusively to the Shamba. There are other tribes who feel and respond to the call of the open. And every year many families, including some of the well-known chiefs, leave their homes and solidly-built palaces to spend the summer months in the low striped tents of their ancestors. But they never range very far afield, and their knowledge of the outlying districts of their own land is not vast. I have been eagerly questioned by chiefs in the north as to the physical conditions of the country and the mode of life prevailing in the south they have never themselves visited.

Though we did not see them in any great quantity until after leaving El-Goléa, for some days we had been putting up small troops of gazelle, dainty little beasts of incredible speed and very difficult to stalk. For these the French Government have instituted a close season, but the Arabs, particularly the nomads, pay little or no attention to it. For them fresh meat is fresh meat, and seeing gazelle always in abundance, they fail to understand the reason for protection.

Hares, too, were common, and with partridges made a welcome addition to the pot; for perpetual hen becomes tedious, and mutton was not procurable, as we had passed no villages since leaving Metlili.

From the north the approach to El-Goléa is through a wide valley twelve miles long, bordered on one side by rock cliffs that rise sheer from the ground, and on the other by rolling sand dunes.

For the whole twelve miles the trail is perfectly straight, with only here and there an isolated bush of stunted *drinn* that accentuates rather than relieves the monotony of the outlook.

And only one ravine cuts through the otherwise wholly unbroken dead-level of the cliff face.

We grew very weary of that long, straight valley that appeared never-ending and to lead to nowhere. And to make the way seem longer, that morning mules and camels alike were slow and stubborn and contrary, as if they had privately agreed amongst themselves overnight to give as much trouble as possible. But for the fact that we knew they were genuinely tired, for rapid travel and bad going had tried them all, there would have been many more tempers lost than were lost before we eventually reached El-Goléa. Kharbouch's camel went completely on strike, lying down every five minutes, roaring with rage, and spitting his cud all over the front of Cookie's clean white gandoura; while my own beast was seized with an insane desire to climb the unclimbable rock face, and kept on breaking away from the line of march and trying in other ways to demoralize his companions.

Towards the middle of the morning a rather fine mirage appeared, an illusory lake with tall palm trees waving above minarets and cupolas that hovered for perhaps ten minutes against the horizon and then vanished, leaving us to wonder whether it was indeed a mirage or El-Goléa itself, hidden again by some inequality of the ground we had not noticed. But it proved to be a mirage, for the cupolas it represented do not exist in El-Goléa; nor, as we afterwards found, could we have seen the town from where we were, as it lies behind a low range of hills.

It was midday before we reached the end of the long valley and, swinging at right angles to follow the line of the hills where they curved abruptly, rode through the scattered palm gardens that form a shady and pleasant suburb to the town.

It was the hour of the siesta when we arrived, and all the people were asleep and within doors.

And passing through the deserted streets, El-Goléa appeared like a village of the dead, so empty and devoid of life it seemed. And even at any other time of day, or at any other season of the year than this, when a large number of the inhabitants are living out in the desert in tents, many of the streets are silent and lifeless, for nowadays El-Goléa is half empty. And unless something is done to stay the steady evacuation that is quietly but surely taking place—and it is difficult to see how the authorities can prevent it—the town in a few years will undoubtedly become wholly deserted. For El-Goléa is a military outpost, and to many of its people the continual presence of the garrison —tiny though it is—is distasteful.

And so it comes about that every year more and more families slip away, never to return.

We camped on the outskirts of the town, close beside the high wall built round the Government Wireless Station. The sight of the tall aerial, and the drone of the dynamos, came as a kind of shock, and seemed strangely out of place in this little desert town. But the constant cutting of the telegraph wires by bandits has made the *télégraphie sans fil* a necessity, and these Wireless Stations now stretch right across the Sahara.

The news of our arrival spread quickly, and almost before the tents were up the whole town arrived en masse.

And until the end of our stay we were never without an excited, jabbering crowd of spectators squatting round the camp in circles, watching and discussing our every movement—which was amusing, but at times embarrassing.

Since they had only once before seen white women, their interest was perhaps excusable—at any rate we thought so. But Kharbouch was deeply shocked, and professed great contempt for the manners of the inhabitants. He voiced his opinion the next afternoon while serving tea. Having had almost to fight his way from the cook tent to the mess tent, he slammed the teapot down on the table, and rushed back to the open doorway to shake his fist in the faces of some of the hardier inquisitives who had crept up close to peep inside. "*Roh, bara!*" he screamed, and a good deal more that is unprintable, and then turned to me with a scornful shrug of the shoulders. "These people are nothing but savages," he said wrathfully. It would have hurt his feelings had he been told that at the moment no one resembled a savage more than himself. Divested of burnous and gandoura—for, like all the men, he had taken advantage of the few days' halt to indulge in a grand and universal wash—he was clad only in black cotton Algerian trousers, a spotted white shirt, a bright yellow shawl folded many times round his waist, and a silk handkerchief of the same gaudy hue tied gipsy fashion round his head. Standing truculently hand on hip, twirling his moustache fiercely and scowling at the temporarily abashed villagers, he needed only the addition of a long, curved scimitar to make him the typical Algerian corsair of the Middle Ages.

"Savages, *awā*," he repeated disdainfully, "as bad as the people of Hind, who are savages indeed, since they worship an animal." This with an air of pride, and a sidelong glance at me to see if I was properly impressed with the extent of his knowledge. But it was too hot to discuss theology, even with Kharbouch, so I gently intimated that some fresh boiling water was of more interest to me just then than the superstitions of the benighted Hindoo.

On the north side of El-Goléa, just beyond the cemetery, is a conical hill of rock crowned with a half-ruined *ksar* which gives the town its name, for El-Goléa means the little castle. Little or nothing seems to be known of the origin of this old fortress, of who built it, or when. The modern Arab appears to take small interest in the activities of his forefathers. "It is old. It has always been," is the invariable reply to questions regarding ancient monuments. And old may mean a hundred, or five hundred years.

Whoever was responsible for its construction had certainly an eye for a commanding situation, for the *ksar* dominates the surrounding country and guards the principal pass through the mountains on the north.

Though no fierce race of warriors remains to issue forth and harry the neighbouring district, the *ksar* is still regarded with awe, and dark mystery

hangs over its ruined battlements. For many
years its only occupant has been a blind woman,
who lives the life of a recluse in some corner of
the vast mass of dwellings.

Never seen, and never putting foot outside her
stronghold, she takes in food that is brought to
her and leaves money in payment on the rock
beside her door. What was once a ramp leading
to the main entrance is now only a narrow track,
overgrown with camelthorn and strewn with
tumbled stones and rock.

And nightfall finds the vicinity of the *ksar*
deserted, for none seem to care to approach it
after dark.

In Algeria superstition plays a very large part
in the lives of the people; malevolent spirits are
thought to lie in wait at every turn to trap the
unwary, and many old women are credited with
being in league with demons. Consequently the
strange secluded life of the blind woman of El-
Goléa is enough in itself to give rise to all manner
of fantastic imaginings; while the nearness of the
mountains, where the djinns and afreets, who are
so intimately bound up with the Arab's creed, are
supposed to be more than ordinarily potent, makes
her association with the powers of darkness seem
all the more probable. The locality, too, is particularly conducive to the idea. For the adjacent
hills are supposed to be a favourite haunt of the
powerful demon Lazerour—known in the north as
Rohania—who feeds on the blood of murdered

men, and to whom are attributed all accidents amongst animals. But though we made a tour of the *ksar* one evening when the shadows of night were closing in, we saw nothing, and heard nothing more alarming than the hoarse croaking of bullfrogs in the marshes round about.

The town itself is not interesting. And the military occupation makes it less so, for each tiny street is labelled with a staring blue-enamelled placard bearing the name of some famous French general, which names are liable to sudden and frequent change to suit the popular hero of the moment, and here look out of place and ridiculous.

Of the few shops left open—most were closed in the absence of their owners—the only one worthy of the name was a little eight-foot-by-six emporium that was full to overflowing with gimcrack trade goods imported from the north, and devoid of most of the common necessaries for which Kharbouch was searching. Even he turned shuddering from the few rusty relics of canned foods. The mosque, too, had nothing to commend it, except a rather graceful minaret.

But what is interesting is the gardens, for El-Goléa has an abundance of water, and anything and everything grows in profusion. Not only native, but European vegetables thrive under cultivation, while northern trees, seen nowhere else in the south, here attain to a great size and age.

We spent the whole of one long hot morning in

THE MOSQUE AT EL-GOLÉA

the garden suburb, wandering from plot to plot, sitting in the cool shade of the palm trees, watching the lazy trickle of little irrigating streams running sluggishly from one open mud channel into another, and chatting with the few gardeners still left in the town. Only a low mud embankment separates the gardens, and here, as everywhere in Algeria, one can roam freely without let or hindrance. One is never shouted at for trespassing, or interfered with in any way. On the contrary, visitors are greeted with a broad smile of welcome, and any word of praise or interest expressed brings the proud proprietor in a twitter of excitement to lead a personally conducted tour through his domain. Glad of any excuse to down tools and rest his weary back, he will chatter by the hour if one is so minded, pleased as a child to show the result of his labours, and delighted to fill one's hands with nosegays of flowers and even branches of blossoms torn from the fruit trees.

The owner is not always present in person; sometimes it is only a servant, Arab or negro, but he does the honours with the same grace and is as lavish as his master in the giving of bouquets. Or it may be an old woman, lean and toothless and incredibly wrinkled, who, timid at first, soon grows garrulous and eventually bold enough to finger and stroke the white women's strange clothing and marvel at their uncovered faces, ignoring in her excitement the fact that her own veil is not so firmly fastened as custom decrees.

CAMPING IN THE SAHARA

And sometimes the only visible workers in a garden will be a group of young girls, slender, graceful little things with mischievous, laughing eyes, who scatter like frightened rabbits at sight of a stranger, and run to hide behind a palm tree or a well-head.

But young girl and toothless hag, proprietor and servant, they toil alike at work that is hard and never-ending. For only by increasing labour are the ever-encroaching sands kept back, the tiny conduits that carry the life-giving water kept open, and the fruits of the earth wrung from a dry and reluctant soil. Early in the morning and far into the evening these gangs of village agriculturists can be met going to and from the gardens that constitute their everything. Here, as in any other country, they work to live. For neglect means a poor harvest, and a failure of crops brings famine.

I have often heard the Arab described as a lazy, worthless animal. In some districts he may be. In others he certainly is not, and I speak of what I have seen. It is unfair to judge the whole race by the wastrels who congregate in and around the northern towns, degenerates who have suffered by a too close association with so-called civilization. There is no comparison between them and the as yet unspoiled Arab of the desert. Hardy and independent, dignified and courteous, these last can only command respect for the arduousness of their lives and the gallant fight they make to maintain existence.

THE GARDEN IN THE WILDERNESS

The most wonderful garden of all was said to be that of the Bureau Arabe, which for many years has been the hobby of the lieutenant in charge.

So constantly was its beauty dinned into our ears that, to satisfy our curiosity, I broke my invariable rule and sent my card to the lieutenant, quite frankly stating my wish to see the wonders of which I had heard so much.

A courteous invitation resulting, we went—and found, like Sheba's Queen, that the half had not been told. For a garden in the desert it was wonderful. The lieutenant, a short, spare, sad-eyed little man, looking like a jockey trained down to the last ounce, welcomed us pleasantly but very shyly.

Quite without the self-satisfied assurance usual among his kind, his painfully nervous manner and slow, jerky speech gave the impression of one who had long lost touch with his own world, and who viewed the arrival of strangers not as a welcome break to the monotony of his life, but as a rather trying ordeal to which courtesy compelled him.

After the exchange of a few polite banalities he suggested a move from his gloomy, somewhat untidy little office to the gardens. Outside in the open, however, and among his treasured trees and flowers, his manner became more easy. And prompted by a few natural questions, he talked readily and with evident pleasure of the work to which he has devoted many years.

CAMPING IN THE SAHARA

We went first to inspect the well, where a simple form of ram raises a never-failing supply of water to a big shallow stone trough, from which it flows through narrow mud channels all over the garden, irrigating the crops. The volume of water is remarkable. Drawn from some underground source, when the elementary mechanism is put into action it rushes up with a roar to the surface and several feet into the air, before it falls back bubbling and foaming into the trough. Even in the severest time of drought this well is said never to fail.

With the addition of an equable climate it is small wonder that the gardens of El-Goléa are lovely. Through groves of orange trees—of a hundred different species—apple trees, plum trees, figs and grenadines, we roamed among great straggling rose bushes, past hedges of jasmine and other flowering shrubs, under canopies of bougain-villæa and climbing vines, to a spot where thousands of huge, long-stemmed purple violets filled the air with a scent that was almost overpowering. It was like a breath of England in the springtime. And smiling at our delight, the lieutenant gathered them recklessly, thrusting great bunches into our hands.

Though distance and lack of facilities prevent their export, the oranges of El-Goléa are famous, said to equal if not excel those of Blidah, and the lieutenant was anxious we should taste them. But the season was nearly over, and only a few hung

THE GARDENS OF EL-GOLÉA

on the trees that were already white with the blossoms of the next crop. Still a few were found to sample, and they were delicious.

Encouraged by our interest, rather tentatively the lieutenant inquired whether we would care to see his vegetable garden.

Keen to see all that El-Goléa could produce, we left the grateful shade of the orange groves and followed him out once more into the brilliant sunshine.

Here again was the same prodigality. What he modestly referred to as his little *jardin potager* looked in reality like a huge market garden, and literally covered acres of ground. Not growing haphazard in patches, as in the native gardens, but planted in orderly rows, each variety enclosed in its own neat square allotment and kept scrupulously free from weeds, were all the vegetables ever mentioned in a cookery book, and a great many more besides—enough to satisfy the needs of a regiment. There was one whole acre, at least, of strawberries—alas, only in bloom—and gooseberry and currant bushes by the hundred. As we wandered from plot to plot the wonder of it became almost more than we could bear in silence, and C. and I looked at each other blankly, the same thought in our minds—what does he do with it all? And the wonder still remains. For though some of the produce, as I found out afterwards, goes to the few White Fathers living in the town, some to the French military doctor, and some to

the three half-caste Algerians who form the per-
sonnel of the Wireless Station, nothing is given to
the native residents, and every year there must be
a tremendous quantity of surplus stuff left to waste
and rot.

Nor is the object of this extensive cultivation
to give labour, for only a very few men are
employed.

Beyond the vegetable plots are vineyards, the
grapes of which make a very good *vin ordinaire*, or
so the owner affirmed. But here, too, the output
must greatly exceed consumption, for the quantity
of vines was amazing.

Attracted by a homely hubbub that in such
a place sounded strangely but pleasantly in our
ears, we left the scene of lavish production and
retraced our steps to the Bureau Arabe.

Skirting the house we crossed an open space
and, passing through a wicket gate, found ourselves in a picturesque tree-shaded farmyard. For
a moment it seemed as if we had been suddenly
transported far from Algeria, for what we saw was
a typical French *basse-cour*.

In a line of lean-to shelters stood sleek, well-
nourished cows—humpbacked cattle from Central
Africa, for northern cows cannot stand the heat—
placidly munching their evening forage; bunched
in a corner of the yard a score of fat white geese
craned their necks and hissed at us angrily; regiments of ducks waddled past, mingling with the
hens that were scratching and squabbling over the

grain that had just been thrown to them; beside little wooden hutches lop-eared rabbits hopped about lazily, nibbling at fresh lettuce leaves, their tiny noses twitching with excitement; while overhead flocks of pigeons circled and swooped, cooing as they came to rest on the tall, old-fashioned dovecot. There were even pigs, clean plump porkers fattening in well-kept styes. And in and about, roaming at will, the inevitable donkey, wailing his disgust of the world in general—though his well-rounded ribs gave no excuse for his discontent.

Leaning on the wall of the pig pens, scratching the back of a slumbering hog with my riding-whip, I discussed stock and stock-breeding with the lieutenant, but my thoughts were with the man himself.

Gardener, agriculturist and farmer, what time had he for the work that was properly his?

In charge of a military outpost, he was a soldier, a cavalry officer, and it is not usual for these commandants to be left to spend the best part of their lives in one station. Yet here everything pointed to a long and continued residence. He spoke of experiments that had taken years to perfect, he sketched plans for the future that would take as long to accomplish.

There seemed to be something very wrong somewhere.

The talk turning on horses, I asked to see his chargers. A smile lit up his face, and with more enthusiasm than he had yet shown he led the way to another part of the establishment, where, in the usual lean-to stables of the country, stood two powerful-looking, bad-tempered black Barbs, kicking and biting at the grooms who were bedding them down for the night.

Bad breaking is responsible for most of the viciousness amongst Arab horses, and it was probably so in this case. But whether it was really vice or merely lightheartedness, the men appeared none too happy with them, and kept a watchful lookout for snapping teeth and iron-shod heels while they were working in the stalls. The lieutenant, however, handled them freely, enumerating their points with pride, and evidently pleased with the praise they were accorded.

Both stallions, five and six years old, short-backed and deep-chested, with muscular loins and quarters and the low-set-on tail that distinguishes a Barb from an Arab, they showed up well when stripped.

Too tall, I thought them, to be quite thoroughbred, but their owner assured me they were *pur sang*, so I had to take his word for it.

Back once more among the shady orange groves, we discussed Algeria, the Hoggar Mountains and the Touareg—of whom he seemed to know much, for he spoke of five years spent amongst them—and many relative matters that showed him to have a far greater knowledge of and a deeper love for the country than has the average military officer. His Arabic, too, was perfect, far above the ordinary standard.

Evening was coming on when we at last reluctantly tore ourselves away from the lovely garden. The lieutenant went with us to the gates of the Bureau Arabe, filling our hands with a parting gift of flowers and, saluting, vanished among the palm trees.

The tragedy of his face haunted me, and I walked back to camp wondering what serpent trailed its dark shadow through the wonders of his beautiful Eden. He had spoken only of the past; not once had the Great War been mentioned. The medals that gleamed on his tunic were the medals of a Moroccan campaign of twenty years ago. He was white-haired, and still only a lieutenant.

With his years of service, his knowledge of the country and its people, his intimate acquaintance with the language, he seemed fitted for a higher command, a more responsible position than lieutenant in charge of a little outpost which, important though it may be, is not of the most important.

Later, when I returned to the north, I learned his history, and the reason for his non-advancement. But that reason is a purely private one that cannot be given here.

A good deal of the famous leatherwork of the Touareg women—specimens of which are found in nearly every Arab house—comes first to El-Goléa, from where it is distributed to the northern dealers. The opportunity, therefore, of acquiring some genuine pieces—without the doubt felt elsewhere that they may be imitations made in some of the ateliers of the White Fathers—was too good to be neglected. So before leaving the town we made another more thorough examination of the unspeakable little shop, and behind some bolts of dusty cotton goods we found one or two really good bits, and carried them off in triumph. But they were a sore trial for the rest of the trip and for long after we reached home. Whether it was the dressing used in curing the skins, or the dyes with which they were coloured, I do not know. But the fact remains they reeked to heaven. And everything packed with them in the same holdall took on the same peculiar and overpowering smell, until we were tempted many times to throw them out and leave them among the sands of the desert.

No description of El-Goléa would be complete without some mention of the curious breed of sheep which are peculiar to that locality. Covered with short coarse hair quite different from the ordinary sheep's fleece, as tall and almost as big as a month-old calf, with long, stilt-like legs and head shaped like a deer's, they have almost no flesh on their bones and are bred solely for their skin, which is very thick and strong and used for all kinds of leatherwork. Very agile, they are more like gazelle than sheep in their movements.

THE GARDEN IN THE WILDERNESS

Droves of them are sent north to be sold, but rarely get farther than the M'Zab Valley.

We saw them first at Ghardaia, where a few exposed for sale in the market-place attracted the attention of our men, who gathered round them in amazement, never having seen the variety before.

At El-Goléa theirs was the only mutton procurable, and lean and tough, it was scarcely worth the cooking.

Throughout our stay, and for some days after leaving El-Goléa, we scanned the surrounding country hoping against hope for the sight of a band of the veiled riders from the Hoggar Mountains. But luck was against us—or, perhaps, for us—and the Hoggar and its white-mounted bandits is still a dream that may yet be for another time.

VII

NOMADS

OUR southernmost point reached, we again avoided caravan routes and, heading in the north-easterly direction, set out for an extended tour through the nomad country. These are the genuine nomads, the true wanderers of the desert who live always in the open, knowing no other home than the low felt tents in which they are born and live and die.

Among them are all kinds, rich and poor, but all alike friendly and hospitable, though many we visited, indeed the majority, had never seen Europeans before.

Untouched by civilization, primitive, hardy and independent, they are the best type of Arab and, physically, the finest specimens of their race.

Their women, too, differ much from the women of the north and the towns, who rarely set foot outside their houses, but spend their days in monotonous idleness in overheated, overcrowded harems.

In the clean fresh air of the desert the nomad women lead a healthier, freer life, that has a marked effect on their appearance. In a word, they wear better. Many we saw were extraordinarily handsome, even the older ones, while some of the young girls were really beautiful. Less timid than the town dwellers, they carry themselves better, and their frank, animated faces show nothing of the bored weariness usual among their more secluded sisters.

Though the wives of the rich nomads are scrupulously veiled, the desert women of the poorer class leave their faces uncovered. Consequently there are amongst the nomads, as also amongst the unveiled Kabyle women, more happy marriages than elsewhere. For, mixing freely together, the young people have opportunity for seeing and getting to know one another, with the result that mutual affection is often the outcome and genuine love-matches are arranged.

But while this freer, unrestricted life undoubtedly improves the physique of the race, it unfortunately tends towards a general laxity of morals. Though not universally immoral, the Arab is constitutionally unmoral. And in a land where girls and boys mature very early, where both are endowed by nature with an ardent temperament, passions run high and the promiscuous mingling of the sexes leads to unbounded licence, which, theoretically condemned, is practically condoned.

Some nomads keep only to one wife, but the majority have two and sometimes three. In defence of this practice Arabs have told me that it is often the first wife herself who suggests to her husband the advisability of adding another "sister" to the family circle, alleging as a reason that, growing older, the head wife begins to feel the burden of children, the household cares, and the spinning and weaving with which she occupies her every spare moment, more than she can accomplish alone, and so she asks for the aid of a younger woman to share her toil.

Such complaisance in any woman seems hardly credible; nor is the reason given really adequate, for the household duties are no greater, indeed very often much less, than those performed by thousands of other women throughout the world. And the richer nomads have certainly no such excuse for polygamy. These can afford and do provide servants, usually negresses, for their wives. The rich nomad augments his harem for his own pleasure and that he may get children, preferably male children.

It is just this same fear of dying without a direct heir born of his own body that prompts some of the highest placed and most enlightened of the Algerian chiefs to take a second wife, should the first wife prove childless.

Usually these highly-placed chiefs are monogamous, not from any scruple, for they see the matter from the standpoint of the Prophet, but for the very simple reason that nowadays even the Arab women have learned to expect and demand very much more in the way of luxury than was thought necessary years ago, and consequently a wife is now far more expensive to keep.

And not all Arab women welcome the arrival of a second wife, or tamely submit themselves to being put on one side. Many of them, devotedly attached to their husbands, fiercely resent the transference of affection and favours that were once wholly theirs, and see in the newcomer only a rival whose youth and beauty will eclipse their own perhaps fading charms and leave them with but the empty title of mistress of the household.

In these divided families the women suffer torments of jealousy and hatred that sometimes lead to terrible tragedies.

The system of very early marriages prevailing among the Arabs—where the bride is often only eleven or twelve years of age, and the bridegroom rarely older than sixteen—is largely responsible for polygamy, for by middle-age the woman is worn out and old from excessive child-bearing, while the man is still in full possession of health and strength. And never very faithful at the best of times, viewing all women merely from a physical standpoint, he sees no reason to mortify the flesh and deny himself what he is yet able to enjoy.

But in spite of all that has been written on the subject, the Arab woman is not altogether the abject and worthless slave of her husband she has been represented. She has rights to which she clings tenaciously, and can insist upon—provided she has male relatives with courage and interest enough to come to her aid and demand that justice be done her. But the need must be very great, and the charge preferred by the husband against his wife be very flagrant, before the woman's relatives will interfere in any matrimonial dispute. For an Arab buys his wife, and her relatives are not readily inclined to refund her purchase money, which they must do should her divorce or repudiation—and there is a big difference between the terms—be caused by any transgression of hers. On the other hand, when an Arab divorces or repudiates his wife to suit his own convenience, he is obliged, conforming to the laws of the Prophet, to provide for her maintenance for the remainder of her life. How many do, and how many do not, is a question open to argument.

Our friend the bandit chief, who had politically effaced himself during the stay in El-Goléa, rejoined us a few miles north of the town. His presence was of great assistance amongst the nomads, for most of them were of his own tribe, and travelling under the auspices of their chief we were assured of a welcome wherever we went.

After the rough going of the previous weeks the easier country we were traversing formed a pleasant change. We had turned our backs to the high bleak Hamada, with its cold and piercing winds; we had seen the last of the rugged, intricate chain of mountains with its grand but gloomy gorges and its hair-raising passes and defiles. The way now led across soft undulating ground; over rolling sand dunes; through great stretches of steppe-like country, gravel-strewn and covered with sparse herbage; and wide shallow depressions, not deep enough to call valleys, that were ringed about with tiny flat-topped hills.

Every day the sun grew hotter, the glare from the sand more intense. And every day we plodded steadily forward through a region where there were no distinctive landmarks, where each successive wind storm that blows must alter the shape of the ever-rolling, ever-slipping sand hills and utterly change the whole aspect of the country. Instinct, and instinct alone, seemed to guide the trackers' feet. And even they, wonderful though they were, were sometimes at fault, so that there were days when we went miles out of our way and remained many hours longer than we bargained for in the saddle.

At such times our only thought was of water, and we began to have a dim idea of what it must be like to be lost, with empty goatskins, in the midst of this vast and arid desolation. It is during these moments of reflection that the forlorn crumble of bones that was once a camel is not the cheeriest spectacle with which to be met. Still even these melancholy fragments have their uses—for where camels have been camels can go, and if one is fated never to arrive, then *in cha Allah*, it is the will of God!

This stretch of waterless country, for wells are few and far between, is called by the Arabs the Land of Thirst. Here only gazelle flourish, the swift little gazelle of the south, whose strange faculty of going without water for long periods enables them to thrive and multiply where no other animal can live; these, and an odd hare or two, an occasional hawk sailing downwind with outstretched, quivering wings, and every now and then a small flock of clumsy lesser bustard, who rise heavily from a cover of scrub to flop a few yards and then settle again, are the only living creatures to be seen.

It might equally well be called the Land of Mirage, for here these optical illusions appeared daily—not only tantalizing, palm-shaded lakes that sparkled temptingly against the horizon, but also what seemed to be whole regiments and armies of galloping horsemen whose wavering, intangible forms we watched through the shimmering heat haze until our eyes grew dim and our heads reeled with dizziness.

Shortly after we turned north to begin the homeward journey Ramadhan began.

For the first few days, until they grew accustomed to the long fast, the men suffered severely. Tasting nothing as they did between sunrise and sunset, it was pitiful to watch them at the mid-

ONE OF OUR CAMPS IN THE NOMAD COUNTRY

day halt lying exhausted on the sand, too parched with thirst even to speak, and all with splitting headaches that made them very unlike their usual cheery selves. It was not so much the lack of food as the lack of water that tried them, for the days were scorching.

We used to feel almost criminal when we ate our own lunch and drank the Evian that had been cooling in a waterskin and of which we had been dreaming all the morning. It was no small consolation that Kharbouch, who prepared and served our food, had himself a dispensation from his priest to postpone his month of fasting to a later and more convenient season. But the men made up for it at night, and gorged at their evening meal.

As we got farther into the heart of their country more and more nomads appeared, and at last rumours reached us of a big sheep-shearing that was going forward among the flocks of one of the richest nomads of the district.

The annual sheep-shearing is always an occasion for much merry-making and gaiety, for at these times a man's friends congregate from far and wide to aid him in the great work, while the fortunate owner keeps open house and feasts his willing helpers royally, which is all the recompense they expect, knowing that he himself will help them when their own turn comes.

Should Ramadhan inopportunely occur at this season, fasting is suspended while the shearing is in progress, and the days of omission are dutifully worked off at some other time, when it can best be fitted in.

There are points in the Mohammedan faith that make it a very practical religion!

Owing to the usual Arab vagueness regarding distance and direction, it was rather difficult to learn just where and when the big shearing was to take place, but we pushed on quickly, questioning every nomad we met and extracting a variety of contradictory information that made our search seem rather like hunting for a needle in a haystack.

In the end we happened upon it quite by chance, and nearly a day earlier than the last garrulous informant had led us to suppose. The result was unfortunate as regards photography. For not expecting to come up with the nomad's camp so soon, C. had succumbed to a number of tempting snapshots that morning, so that when we arrived at the scene of operations her pockets were bulging with exposed films, the camera was empty, and all the spare rolls were miles away and unget-at-able on the back of one of the baggage camels.

The nomad's camp was picturesquely situated in a round, shallow depression ringed about and sheltered by low sandhills. A number of black tents were pitched at the foot of the sandhills, decorously removed from too close a proximity to the activities that were taking place in the middle of the little, circus-like depression.

It was an animated scene of frank light-heartedness and good comradeship.

Men and boys, burnouses flung back and arms bare to the shoulders, all talking and laughing at the tops of their voices, were falling over one another in their haste, while they wrestled with the frightened, sad-eyed sheep who were still waiting to be rid of their heavy fleece; excited negro servants, snapping their fingers and screaming shrilly, pranced about with no particular aim in view; and, getting in everybody's way, tiny toddlers of both sexes, rolling and tumbling amongst their elders' feet, added their high-pitched cries to the general uproar.

Supervising them all, the rich nomad, a tall, stalwart fellow with the most jovial face, moved from group to group, beaming with pleasure and radiating hospitality. Already in the highest spirits, the unexpected coming of his chief seemed to be the last drop that filled his cup of happiness to overflowing. Having first humbly kissed his hand, he wrapped his mighty arms round the little man and gave him a regular bear's hug, from which the chief emerged breathless, but smiling.

We were hardly out of the saddle before mint tea arrived. It was never more welcome, and we squatted in a circle on the ground to try and wash the sand and dust out of our throats. In the excitement of the moment Mohammed, our principal tracker, who was taking Ramadhan very seriously, forgot the restrictions of the fasting season and swallowed off a glassful. And when, amidst roars of laughter, some of the others twitted him, he blushed scarlet and, overcome with confusion, hid his face in his hands like a child caught in some naughtiness.

The actual shearing was done inside a semi-circular enclosure—just strips of tent felt strained round wooden posts driven into the ground—that sheltered the workers from the light breeze that was blowing and the drifting sand.

Inside the enclosure dozens of panting sheep lay on their sides, their feet bound, their heads held down by important-looking small boys. And beside each sheep the shearer sat cross-legged, intent on his work, but not too busy to chatter continuously, every man vying with his neighbour to remove the heavy fleece in one unbroken mass.

Though some of them were using big, clumsy-looking scissors, the majority clung to the old-fashioned knife, a thin, curved, blade shaped like a sickle. It seemed a most unsuitable tool, and one likely to cause injury to the sheep. But the men were dexterous, and the few slight cuts I saw were made by the scissors, not by the knife.

The blades of both scissors and knives, which have to be razor-edged, dull quickly, and two men were busily employed all the time sharpening them on whetstones.

One of the most skilful shearers was a man of over ninety, a jolly old patriarch who was full of fun and obviously delighted both with his age and his own dexterity. He inquired most anxiously if we had been told the number of his years, and held up a skinny arm to show how strong he still was.

The work had been going on for some days, and the nomad pointed with pride to huge bales of wool that were stacked in a corner of the enclosure.

These desert sheep, in spite of the scanty herbage and the miles they must travel to procure it, are big, sturdy animals, and grow an extraordinary thick coat which is very fine in texture and of the purest white.

When we had seen the shearing in all its stages, C. and I set off to pay a call on the nomad's wife, escorted by one of the negresses, who danced about in a perfect frenzy of excitement, shrieking out the tidings of our coming.

As we neared the largest tent, the hanging flaps were thrown up and two or three women appeared on the threshold. But one glance at our masculine riding kit sent them scurrying back again with shrill cries of dismay. Doubled up with laughter, the negress screamed reassuring explanations, and once more they gathered in the doorway, smiling shyly and all agog with curiosity, the head wife, who was gorgeously dressed in flowing robes of black and scarlet, standing slightly in advance of the others.

The next moment we were inside the tent,

shaking hands all round, and trying to explain ourselves and our unexpected appearance.

Never having seen Europeans before, they were wildly excited at what was evidently the event of their lives, and crowded round us, all talking at once, so that we could hardly hear ourselves speak above the babel of voices.

News of our visit was sent to the adjacent tents, and more and more women came to swell the throng, until the principal tent was packed full. There must have been at least forty of them, with children and babies galore.

By degrees the head woman asserted her superiority and took charge of the situation. Signing to us to sit down, she took her place near us, while the others sat or knelt round in a close circle.

Our fair complexions and the absence of kohl on our eyes came in for a good deal of comment. But it was our clothes that intrigued them most. Clearly they thought them the funniest things they had ever seen. Patting and stroking them timidly at first, they at length grew bolder and insisted on a thorough examination. Our gloves were already going the round and, their use explained, being tried on amidst shrieks of laughter. Helmets and riding coats went before we could raise a finger in protest. But when we found eager hands wrenching at our shirts to strip them off, and a couple of determined matrons hauling at our long boots, we had to explain as kindly as possible that the entertainment could go no further.

But it was all done in the friendliest fashion. And though it was somewhat embarrassing, their childlike curiosity was so naïve, their interest so perfectly natural, that we could not be other than amused at their inquisitiveness. So we all laughed together, and our scattered garments having been reluctantly restored, we in our turn admired their clothes.

Those who had the finest jewels were most anxious we should not miss seeing anything of their splendour, and rings and brooches, anklets and bracelets were proudly exhibited. There are fashions in jewellery in Algeria as elsewhere. The Kabyle women of the north pride themselves on wearing only silver ornaments, while women of the south prefer gold; but in north and south alike most women wear somewhere about their person a Hand of Fatma, a trinket of gold or silver crudely shaped to represent the five extended fingers of the mother of the Prophet, which is a charm to bring good luck and avert the evil eye.

They were disappointed at our own lack of personal adornment—and our command of Arabic not being sufficient to make them fully understand customs other than their own, I am sure their friendly hearts grieved at what must have seemed to them a mark of great poverty in their strangely attired guests—but they fastened eagerly on my

wedding ring, and were much interested when I
.explained its significance.

The superior rank of our hostess—for the other
women were obviously relatives of lesser degree
and the wives of neighbours come to help with
the sheep-shearing—was shown in her more
elaborate and expensive clothing and in the mass
of jewellery with which she was covered.

Seemingly about twenty-five, she was a beautiful
creature with fine, delicately-cut features and
wonderful dark-brown eyes. She looked very
happy, and was evidently a great favourite with
all present. A very gracious hostess, she played
her part with a pretty little air of dignity when
the inevitable mint tea arrived.

Before that came, however, we had had to
submit to the polite custom of the country, and
had both been drenched with the contents of a
large bottle of scent, so that for the rest of the
visit we sat in a combined odour of attar-of-roses
and mint, which, added to the heat of the tent,
was slightly overpowering. But there was no
other odour to offend even the most fastidious
nostrils. In spite of the crowd that thronged
about us, there was no closeness, no offensive
smell of any kind, nor did we take away with us
any reminders of our stay amongst the primitive
desert people.

The mother-love amongst Arab women is
intense, and many babies were brought to be
admired and tiny boys and girls ranged up to be

shown off. They were strong, healthy-looking
children, and I saw very few cases of ophthalmia
amongst them.

Some of the little boys, already conscious of
their superiority as representing the dominant sex,
were inclined to give themselves airs. But retri-
bution followed swiftly, and one cheeky youngster,
who was making himself particularly objectionable,
having been sent out of the tent two or three
times ineffectually, was finally definitely removed
by a sturdy negress, who marched him off
howling.

It was only during the momentary respite of
tea-drinking that we were allowed any time in
which to take stock of our surroundings. Arab
etiquette demands that the national beverage be
drunk ceremoniously and with due attention to
its flavour. So silence reigned for a few minutes,
whilst the ladies of the harem—and several other
harems—slowly sipped their three glasses, their
eyes fixed unblinkingly upon us the while.

Many of them, besides our hostess, were very
good-looking, with quantities of glossy brown hair
and well-shaped little hands and feet. Nearly all
appeared to be slender, but their voluminous
garments gave them a clumsy look and prevented
any true estimation of their figures.

The tent was long and narrow, and only about
eight feet high. Made of the usual dark-coloured,
felt-like material, it was draped inside with bright
hangings, the floor spread with a big and very

beautiful rug in which reds and blues predominated. Our appreciation of this rug gave great pleasure, and we could see by the head woman's smile and the quick look of pride she flashed at her friends that it was evidently a treasured possession. A few more rugs, rolled up, and embroidered leather cushions completed all the furnishings. Being a rich man's home, there was another inner room, screened from the big outer apartment by more curtains. Into this we did not penetrate, but, judging from the size of the tent, it must have been as long, though not as broad as the reception-room.

When the time came to leave them, the women were very loath to let us go, and it took a good deal of explaining before we could persuade them that we could not stay on indefinitely.

We got away at last after more handshaking, and left them crowded in the doorway of the tent, waving to us and calling down God's peace and innumerable blessings on our heads.

The temptation to remain longer amongst these simple, friendly desert folk was great, particularly as the nomad himself had already begged us to camp with them for a few days to see the end of the festivities. But we had many other camps yet to visit, and unfortunately time would not allow of too long a stay in any one place.

Also by this time the caravan had long since passed, and was too far away to be recalled. Indeed, so far away was it that we almost lost it altogether, and very nearly had to spend the night without food or tents. Just because it was a time when we wanted the baggage camels to travel slowly, the perverse creatures—and their equally perverse drivers—elected to do a record march, and went miles farther than had been arranged. The ground, too, was difficult for the trackers, and after a few hours' riding we lost the spoor of the caravan completely and had to guess the direction it had taken.

When sunset came we had not yet found the tracks, and were dolefully reckoning up the fragments that remained in the lunch basket.

The evening was hot and windless, and we had the saddle blankets if the worst came to the worst, so a night without shelter would not have hurt us. But the desert is a desperately hungry place !

It was a beautiful stretch of country—rolling sand dunes that glowed bright pink in the light of the setting sun, with here and there solitary shafts of red, friable rock towering skywards like tall monuments, and not very far away the dark smudge of a chain of low hills of the same soft red rock.

Overhead the deep blue sky was fading to a band of jade green on the horizon, where the sun, like a fiery ball, was going down in a riot of crimson and gold. Slowly the light went, the blue sky became almost black, and one by one the stars came out.

Scattered widely apart, but keeping within

shouting distance of each other, the few men with us searched the ground for traces of the lost caravan, until at last a joyful hail from somewhere in the dusk announced that the imprint of camels' feet had been found and recognized as our own. And a few minutes later, topping a high dune, we fell in with some of the camel drivers, who had already got the tents up and were just setting out to look for us.

There was a well near by, the Hassi Ouled Mohamed, and as we had a stretch of waterless country ahead of us, the men were up half the night filling waterdrums and goatskins. We walked down after dinner to watch them.

Three large fires of brushwood lit up the busy scene round the well-head, making darker the pitch blackness of the surrounding night, and throwing odd flickering shadows among the men as they toiled at the ropes with a rhythmical chant of *Ya, ya,* that ended in a deep grunt of relief when they pulled the dripping goatskins clear of the parapet.

In a great circle round the well, imperfectly seen in the darkness, lay big shapeless forms that looked like sand-heaps, until a vicious snarl and a snapping of teeth discovered them to be kneeling camels. Having a few minutes before threaded a hazardous passage through our own bad-tempered beasts, the presence of these other camels was intriguing, but the fires burning up suddenly, we saw many strange faces round the

NOMADS ROUNDING UP SHEEP TO MILK

well, and realized that a party of nomads had come to the *hassi* on the same errand as ourselves.

One of the nomad lads had a flute, and he and Lakada piped against each other vigorously, keeping time to the chanting of the men.

Journeying between the various nomad camps we frequently met men and youths, who had been away trading or helping with the sheep-shearing, searching for their families amongst the sand dunes. These often joined us for an hour or so during the day, glad to see others in the wilderness and have company on their way. One of them told us that he had been searching for weeks and could hear no tidings of his own people, who had moved to other pastures in his absence.

At one of the camps the nomads tried to sell us a baby gazelle, about six weeks old, which had just been caught by some of the boys. It was a pretty little creature with great, frightened eyes, and fast already on its feet. But it was impossible to take it with us as a pet, and Kharbouch scornfully rejecting it as too small for the pot, we had to leave it behind, where it doubtless found an end in the cous-cous of the less discriminating nomads.

Having failed to get a photograph of the sheep-shearing, we were fortunate in having the camera fully charged when we came upon another large camp where the sheep were being rounded up to be milked.

Here the people were neither so rich nor so high

in rank as the great flock master, and men and women were mixing freely as they drove in the sheep and tied them, heads together, in bunches of nine and ten.

After the milking was over we went with them to inspect their tents and watch the women spinning and weaving. These desert women never seem to have their hands empty. With a baby astride of one hip they go about their various tasks, never ceasing to twirl the primitive spindle from which they draw the yarn that is ultimately woven into burnouses, tent-cloth and rugs. Sheep's wool, camel and goat hair are all used, and serve different purposes.

The tents were less luxurious than those of the rich nomads, some being little more than mere shelters of brushwood with a sparse covering of old and faded felt. But they were cheery folk, apparently quite contented with their lot, and there was certainly no sign of race suicide amongst them, for the camp was swarming with children.

Hospitable as are all the desert people, they brought as refreshment crushed dates and lumps of sour cheese. But we were able to decline their kindly-meant offerings without giving offence by saying that we had just eaten, an excuse that is always accepted. Both cheese and butter made from sheep's milk are terribly rank, and we were already far too well acquainted with the flavour, for our tinned butter had long since given out and all the cooking was being done with sheep's milk butter, so that the nauseating taste of it was always in our mouths.

But what is quite palatable is a little brown species of truffle found in the nomad district. Growing a few inches below the level of the sand, they resemble small potatoes in shape, and are quite good to eat after being well washed and cooked in butter. Only a tiny depression in the sand marks their presence, and I could never find them. But the men seemed to know instinctively where they were, and scooped them up by dozens as they went along.

Mushrooms also grow freely. But these we had to leave untasted, for the men were as foreign to that neighbourhood as we were, and, so many of the varieties in Algeria being poisonous, no Arab will touch a mushroom outside his own district.

Though they have large flocks of sheep and goats, the nomads rarely eat the flesh of either; their milk, with the butter and cheese made from it, is used, but they are principally bred for their wool and hair.

In the desert camels also are considered too valuable for food, and are only eaten when an accident has made them useless for further work.

But when meat is required—and an Arab will always eat meat when he can get it—there is an unfailing supply of gazelle and, in spite of it being the close-season, every nomad camp we passed had fresh-killed gazelle meat in plenty which the nomads were ready and anxious to sell.

And all through the nomad country we saw gazelle by the thousand, sighting troop after troop all day and every day, and watched them as they fled from us in great circles, leaping through the air with long, graceful bounds and running like the wind.

Shy, wild and hardy, these little creatures are the embodiment of the very spirit of the wilderness, and in their constant flight and roving habit the true nomads of the desert.

THE HEAVENLY TWINS

VIII

OUARGLA AND A NIGHT MARCH

PLODDING slowly towards it, over an immense Chott which took all the afternoon to cross, Ouargla seemed to be an illusive town. Since midday seen faintly against the skyline, it appeared to recede from us with every step we took forward. Hours passed and still the dark line of its palm trees looked just as intangible, just as far away.

The start that morning had been an early one but by seven o'clock the sun was already scorching and the heat rising in great waves to our faces up from the burning sand.

And though we were on high ground and mounting steadily, if imperceptibly, for the gradient was very slight, no breeze came to cool the air and give a momentary respite from the heat.

During the morning the way led over shallow sand dunes, where the men kept a sharp look-out for the poisonous vipers and scorpions that were just beginning to emerge from their winter sleep.

By degrees the dunes, still keeping their shape, changed from soft sand to hard gravel. Then gradually they grew smaller and wider apart, until

167

at last they flattened out into a huge rocky plateau.

The plateau ended abruptly in a sheer cliff face, from which we looked down over the long, wide valley that stretched flat and unbroken miles away to Ouargla. And the whole valley is one large Chott.

Seen at midday from the top of the cliff it was dazzling, for in the fierce glare of the sun the dry salt glistened white as snow.

The long ride across it in the afternoon was sheer misery, that left us half-blinded and with cracked and bleeding lips. Fortunately for the caravan, there was an opening in the cliff face, a weathered passage between huge red boulders, down which we slithered and slipped to the floor of the valley.

In a patch of shade at the foot of the rocks we stopped for a short siesta, leaving the caravan to go forward alone. Had we known the full extent of that deceptive valley there would have been no siesta, nor would we have let the caravan go on without us.

Though the whole length of the Chott is scored with dozens of parallel tracks made by the passing of countless caravans, the thick crust of salt is too hard to show the imprint of a single camel train.

Camels and men were out of sight when we began that long, blinding ride. And as it was dark when we reached the end of the Chott and started over the sandy two miles that still separated us from Ouargla, we had no idea where, in all the big, straggling town with its many suburbs, to look for them.

In the end, after groping our way through gardens that seemed interminable and into blind alleys that led to nowhere, we stumbled upon them quite by accident.

It was pitch black by this time, and we could easily have passed them by unnoticed, and gone wandering round Ouargla for the rest of the night.

But though we could not see them we heard them, and heard them to some purpose.

It was pandemonium let loose, with individual voices we recognized soaring high above the general babel.

Not a tent was up, not a single camel had its load removed, and not a man made a step in that direction, while they argued and shouted and cursed in the darkness, each one blaming the other for what was the united stupidity of them all.

It transpired that while crossing the Chott some bright soul had suggested the taking of what appeared to be a short cut, the fatal short cut that always proves the longest in the end, with the result that they went miles out of their way and had arrived only a few minutes before ourselves.

Our coming merely piled more fuel on the fire.

To the general wrangling was added the wrath

of Kharbouch and the rest of our personal servants, who in their own annoyance and in zeal for our comfort literally fell on the disputants tooth and nail.

For a moment or two it looked as if somebody was going to get hurt.

But a few words from Si A. S. quelled the uproar and set the men sullenly at work.

In the circumstances, since there was nothing we could do and the sight of us waiting was only moving Kharbouch to further explosions of rage, we judged it better to fade quietly away and leave them to it.

After half an hour's wandering we found the main streets, and eventually a small café. It seemed to be the resort of the French garrison quartered in the town, but the *patronne* gave us a quiet room upstairs, where the unmelodious singing of the soldiers echoed only faintly, and supplied unlimited tea and biscuits and jam.

Things had settled down more or less harmoniously when we got back to camp, though dinner was not ready until ten o'clock.

Having had a long and tiring day, nearly twelve hours in the saddle, we decided to go to bed directly afterwards. But the good resolution was frustrated, for half-way through dinner there came a pressing invitation from the Cadi—the chief magistrate of the town—to drink tea with him at his house.

It was then nearly eleven o'clock, but to Arabs,

who habitually sit up gossiping until the early hours of the morning, the night was still young, and it was more politic to go when we were asked rather than suggest a postponement of the visit.

So once more we set off to the town, guided this time by one of the Cadi's servants who had been sent to show the way.

The Cadi of Ouargla, like all Algerian chiefs and public officials, combines commerce with his magisterial duties. So we were not surprised when we reached the house, which is in the heart of the town, to be conducted first through a large store —where even at that late hour a few customers lingered—before plunging into a dark, narrow passage-way that led to the private apartments.

Following the servant, who walked ahead with a lantern swinging in his hand, we went for what seemed the length of several houses, the passage turning and twisting in the most confusing manner, until we reached a long flight of steps, at the bottom of which was a big vaulted chamber where the Cadi and a few of his friends were waiting to receive us.

The dimly-lit room with its high groined ceiling, its pillared archways, its shadowy recesses filled with mysterious-looking bales and bundles, was like the setting for an Arabian Night's tale. Only one corner was adequately lighted. Here a fine rug was spread, with cushions to serve as seats, and we sat down with the Cadi and his little group of friends to mint tea and conversation.

But though the bluff, hearty Cadi was the embodiment of the matter-of-fact, it was one of the most unreal hours I have ever experienced.

Perhaps I was over-tired, so that what was really only unusual became unconsciously exaggerated into the unreal; perhaps it was merely the subdued and rather peculiar lighting effect that stimulated extravagant imaginings, but the whole atmosphere of the place was curious and vaguely disturbing. An occasional figure emerging unexpectedly from behind one of the dark arches kept one's senses constantly on the alert, wondering what next the gloomy, cave-like recesses might reveal, what strange apparition might suddenly flit into view between the tall pillars.

But after tea we settled down to steady talk that left no time for further foolish fancies.

The Cadi, proud of his native town and eager to supply all information, rattled off statistics at amazing speed, of which all I can remember is the fact that Ouargla and its adjacent suburbs number 25,000 souls.

The figure seems rather high, since neither Touggourt nor Biskra boasts so many inhabitants, but the Cadi had no reason to mislead me, nothing to gain by overstating the population. And later, when I saw the extent of the town and its environs, I judged that the census might very well be accurate—as accurate as any census can be in a Mohammedan country.

Much trade passes through Ouargla and it is a

A STREET IN OUARGLA

big caravan centre for goods coming from the north and south.

So commercially important is the town that for some years there has been talk of a railway between it and Touggourt. But nothing has been done yet to realize this scheme, and Touggourt still remains railhead. And it is extremely doubtful whether, in existing circumstances, such a line would pay. For freights in Algeria are high, and the majority of Arab traders still prefer to entrust their goods to the slower-moving but cheaper camel caravans. For military purposes this extension from Touggourt to Ouargla may eventually be put through, but it will be a bad financial speculation for the Government.

Ouargla, its people, and its commerce having been thoroughly discussed, the conversation turned to our own journey, in which the Cadi and his friends were much interested.

Like many other high-placed Arabs with whom I have talked, the Cadi deeply regretted the lack of enterprise that keeps the dominant nation in Algeria from any more extensive knowledge of the land it governs, and leaves to the English and to Americans the pleasure of exploring the outlying districts of this fascinating country.

We spoke of El-Goléa, from which we had just come, and of the temptation that the vicinity of the Hoggar Mountains had been to us. From the Hoggar we arrived by natural sequence at the Touareg and their lawless propensities.

CAMPING IN THE SAHARA

Wishing to see how far the Cadi would concur with statements regarding the tranquillity of the Sahara lately published in a pamphlet written by a recently retired French general, I quoted the following paragraphs : " I venture to assert that as long as we are in the Algerian Sahara no apprehension need be felt with regard to security, for the Pax Gallica prevails right down to the Algero-Soudanese frontier. . . . We may therefore, without the slightest hesitation, travel through the dunes of the Souf and the endless plains of the Sahara, the mountains of the Hoggar, right down to the Soudanese frontier. . . . I can therefore boldly assert that the Sahara is open to tourists. . . . "

Determined for once to try and get a direct answer from an Arab, I asked the Cadi point-blank whether, in his opinion, the Touareg are so peacefully disposed towards tourists, or even traders, as the sanguine general would have us suppose.

The Cadi laughed, then patted the shoulder of a shy little man sitting next him who had not opened his mouth all evening.

" If you want to know about the Touareg, ask my cousin here." The cousin blushed scarlet and tried to hide behind his burly relation. But urged on by the Cadi's encouraging pokes and the insistence of his friends, he coughed deprecatingly and began in a rapid monotone to tell his story of experiences among the Touareg. It was a plain, unvarnished little tale, which the teller seemed to think in no way extraordinary.

Three years ago he left Ouargla, one of a party of traders, to journey to the Hoggar with a camel caravan of trade goods. Their way lay through El-Goléa and In-Salah. Shortly after leaving In-Salah a band of scouting Touareg swooped down on the caravan, killed some of the traders, and carried off the rest—of whom he was one—to slavery in the Hoggar Mountains. For two years he worked as a slave among the Touareg. But though a slave, he was not ill-treated by his master, perhaps because he philosophically settled down to make the best of a bad business. Being an educated man, he was at length taken from manual labour and given secretarial work in connection with the business affairs of the tribe. This brought him into touch with people who were willing to help him, and gave him the opportunity for which he had been hoping. And last year, with the connivance of his master, who had become attached to him, he managed to escape and make his way back to Ouargla.

From this man's story, the truth of which is beyond question, it would seem that there is still a certain measure of risk for traders who venture to do business with the Veiled People.

For the mere traveller, the manner of his reception depends, I think, on the particular district visited, the temper of the people at the moment, and, very largely, on the traveller himself and his method of approaching and dealing with these autocrats of the desert.

I once heard a French officer say that France holds the Hoggar in the hollow of her hand. She may do—but the wily Touareg still seem to slip through her fingers very easily.

One other little fact I would like to record. At the time of my last trip into the Algerian Sahara the general of the pamphlet was also camping there. Was it only in virtue of his late office, I wonder, that he was accompanied throughout his journey by a guard of *goumiers* ?

It was midnight when we left the Cadi and walked back to our camp on the outskirts of the town.

But though the dark streets were deserted, Ouargla was not asleep. Lights still shone in many upper windows ; from behind closed doors came the ceaseless hum of conversation, the rattle of dominoes, the twanging of musical instruments ; and, every now and then, a man's clear tenor voice rang out through the silent night, singing a nomad's love song.

Seen by daylight the principal streets of Ouargla appear uninteresting. The market-place is big, but not particularly individual in style.

Besides Soudanese, and a detachment of Spahis, there is a company of French soldiers quartered in the town. These seem to have little else to do than lounge about the streets in dirty undress uniform.

THE MARKET-PLACE IN OUARGLA

Ouargla is largely populated by the descendants of Soudanese slaves. Since the official abolition of slavery in Algeria these former slaves have by toil and thrift grown rich, and have not only acquired property, but have also freely intermarried with the former owners of the land. Consequently the majority of the inhabitants of the town are more negroid than Arab in appearance, having darker skins, less regularity of feature, and distinctly woolly hair. Their African descent is also shown in their inquisitive curiosity, which is unmitigated by the natural air of dignity which tempers the curiosity of even the most inquisitive Arab.

Straggling out beyond the French soldiers' barracks, public buildings, and market-place—which are all cramped together in the centre of the town—the rest of Ouargla is just an ordinary overgrown Arab village, teeming with people, and with no distinctive feature of any kind. There is more of interest in any one of the many little villages lying round it than in the main town itself.

To one of these villages—Beni-Thoer—we walked one afternoon, a long, tiring tramp over loose sand during which we were nearly devoured by mosquitoes.

In Beni-Thoer the people are more purely Arab, and their interest did not take the offensive form of trying to stare one out of countenance as do the people of Ouargla.

Coming back we made a detour to see the two

M   177

new barracks recently built on the outskirts of Ouargla. One is still empty ; a small detachment of Spahis occupy but do not nearly fill the other.

Our camp was not far from this last building, and throughout our stay the Spahis lost no opportunity of riding their horses up and down and flaunting their long red cloaks past the tents.

When we got back to camp from Beni-Thoer the men, with much laughter, showed us a fine upstanding ram they had bought that afternoon in the market. The animal had been purchased to make good the boast of two of the camel drivers, who declared they could prepare a better *meshwe* than even the Caid of Hadjïera had given us.

Tethered in the meantime to a tent-peg, the ram was to march with the caravan until the auspicious moment arrived for its slaughter. The two men came in for a good deal of chaff that evening, especially from Kharbouch, who was rather piqued at the prospect of rivals in his own particular line of business. But Ben Haoua and Hama' Seghir remained imperturbable and ignored the jeering comments of their comrades.

When the time came to leave Ouargla it seemed strange not to see our bandit friend and his lieutenant preparing with the other men for the march. In the weeks they had travelled with us we had come to know them well, and to appreciate highly the kindly service they had done us.

In their stead we had an unexpected addition to the caravan. This was Maama Xime, the ex-

goumier and merry soul who, almost at the outset of the trip, had been sent by the Caid of the Said-Ouled-Amor to escort us to Hadjïera. Having come down to Ouargla to sell camels, he was on the point of returning home to Touggourt when he heard of our arrival in the town, and rushed off at once to join the camp, where he was received with open arms, for all our men were old friends of his.

For the remainder of the trip, besides enlivening the whole party, he acted voluntarily as additional personal servant. And we were very glad of his help, for Lakada was still hors-de-combat from the bad toss he had taken from the fractious *mahari*.

No camel ever foaled could have thrown Maama Xime, and during the time he travelled with us we learned many new ways of dealing with these refractory beasts.

It was another scorching morning when we left Ouargla and started off over rolling sand dunes that lasted all the way to Touggourt.

As always after a few days' rest, all the beasts were disinclined for work. But in any case it was too hot to hurry, so we jogged on slowly and left the animals to make their own pace. Everything we looked at we saw distorted through a shimmering heat haze that made palm trees appear to be waltzing madly round each other, while tiny sand dunes loomed large as mountains and even the low *drinn* bushes took on gigantic size. Perspective and all sense of proportion go by the board in this kind of atmosphere. An object apparently a mile away leaps to within a few feet almost in the moment of looking at it ; while, conversely, some special point in the landscape that seems near at hand may take an hour's hard riding to reach.

We halted for an hour outside L'Gouca, a sad little tumble-down village where the people all seemed listless and, like ourselves, overcome with the heat. Once it must have been a large and flourishing community, for there were many uninhabited houses now falling into ruins, many evidences of past cultivation that were sanded over and fast going back into desert. Probably in a few years it will be wholly deserted, and another abandoned village will be added to the large number that already lie scattered all over the Sahara.

The only object of interest in L'Gouca was a date palm, the tallest I have ever seen. Even the men, all of them intimately associated with the date industry, were surprised at its size and, reckoning from the rings on the rough trunk, they put its age at over two hundred years.

The sun seemed hotter than ever when we pushed on again. Only the little sand-grey lizards seemed to enjoy the heat, and the ground was alive with them. Darting here and there in short panicky rushes, they lost their heads completely when the caravan approached, scattering blindly in all directions, sometimes running right under the animals' feet, making the camels kick madly, for they hate the feel of the cold, wriggling little bodies against their sensitive pads. Even the heavy, hurrying dung beetles, whose zig-zag trails score every sandy hillock, seemed less busy than usual, sitting meditatively in the line of march, indifferent to a momentary burial when some heavy hoof crushed them into the sand, for they would dig themselves out in a moment or two and hurry away apparently none the worse.

These big beetles (they are an inch long and nearly as broad) always scent a camp, and come in hundreds to pick up any unconsidered trifle. They are quite fearless and have a tenacity of purpose that is beyond praise, for when thrown out of a tent they will reappear again and again, so that sometimes the ground sheet is black with them. They have, too, a liking for climbing up the inside of a tent, and though they fall a dozen times, still they will patiently climb again. In a mess tent it is amusing to watch their heroic struggles, in a sleeping tent the joke quickly palls, for they are very hard and horny and give a nasty pinch if they land on you. Their heavily armoured backs protect them from most things, but they have one enemy, another beetle-like creature of twice their size with a tapering wasp waist and a broad white streak down his black back, who pursues and devours them relentlessly. To these we did object, for they are savage little things who seem to go for one deliberately just for the mere fun of it, and having once got a hold they hang on like a bulldog, and their pinch is a bad one. They are very tenacious of life and hard to kill. Even when cut in two the separated halves carry on independently as if nothing had happened, and they sometimes live for days in this state.

It was now the nesting season, and scores of larks fluttered mutely from *drinn* bush to *drinn* bush; they are paler in colour than the English lark, and I have never heard them sing in the desert. One flew off her nest right in a camel driver's face, and he came grinning to me with two little white eggs lying in the palm of his brown hand.

One other village we passed that first day out from Ouargla, the last we were to see before getting into Touggourt. It too was partly ruined and wholly depressed-looking, and its people were not merely listless but sullen—the only sullen Arabs I have ever met in Algeria.

We stopped at the well to water the animals, and though several men were sitting near there were no cheery greetings such as we were accustomed to, no response to our own men's remarks, no interest of any kind displayed. They might all have been deaf mutes for any sound they made.

As we found them so we left them, sitting dejected in the sunshine—and crossed off Bour as an unamiable locality never to be revisited.

A CONCERT IN THE COOK TENT

After leaving Bour we turned aside from the caravan route, not touching it again until we reached Touggourt.

Our purpose was to visit more nomad encampments, and these are not found very close to any recognized trail.

The way lay through typical nomad country: rolling sand dunes, and long stretches of undulating plain densely covered with camel thorn, big clumps of *drinn*—which looks like esparto grass—and tight little grey-green bushes to which the Arabs give no name, though they are common in many parts of the country.

Everywhere the vegetation showed signs of the rain that had fallen in such quantity several weeks before. And everywhere camels, sheep and goats were grazing by the hundred.

They were days of constant interest, constant delight, but hot days that made for slow progress.

To save the animals somewhat, and to make up a little for lost time, we decided on a night march, which a full moon made possible.

That afternoon we camped early, about three o'clock, pitching only a couple of tents. Here, the men agreed, was the proper time to sacrifice the ram. And the preparation of that *meshwe* took the whole of the rest of the afternoon. Ben Haoua and Hama' Seghir, to make good their boast, were the chief cooks, but everybody assisted.

The animal killed, skinned and cleaned, two

men held the spitted carcase over the glowing red embers of a big wood fire, revolving it slowly, while others basted it, first with salt and water, then with liquid butter. Two hours it took to cook. And every twenty minutes the two men holding the spit had to give place to two others, unable any longer to endure the heat of the fire. At the outset, Kharbouch, his nose in the air, affected supreme indifference. But little by little, as the savoury smell of the roasting meat rose to his nostrils, he began to unbend, until at last, his sleeves tucked up, he was basting away with the best of them.

Dinner was a function that night, with the *meshwe* as the *pièce de résistance*. For the occasion, table and chairs were abolished, and we squatted Arab-fashion on the ground to do justice to the Arab meal.

Afterwards, rolled in saddle blankets, we slept for a couple of hours. And at midnight we were roused.

At first, in the semi-darkness, for the moon was still low, it all seemed hopeless confusion. Ghostly figures sped here and there rounding up already laden camels that were, as usual, straying away by themselves in all directions; more ghosts strained and tugged at the mess tent we had just vacated; close to where C. and I sat holding the mules a *mahari* was fighting Mohammed, who was trying to slip a halter over its snapping jaws; and blundering in from every side, camels stalked past, looking unnaturally large in the dim light.

But the confusion was only apparent, and in a remarkably short space of time we got away, the caravan first, ourselves bringing up the rear.

After the grilling days of sunshine the night air struck cold, and topcoats and burnouses were a necessity.

Travelling by night is altogether different from the usual leisurely progress made by day. Not straggling widely apart, nor stopping to crop the herbage as they do in the daytime, the camels, bunched closely together, slip along swiftly, their necks craned forward, their long limbs swinging in rhythmical step.

The utter silence of the desert by night is one of its greatest wonders, one of its chiefest charms. This night it seemed more than usually silent.

The dry shuffle of the camels' cushioned pads, the quick patter of the mules' feet, the soft murmur of the men's voices, were the only sounds that broke the stillness.

Not light enough yet to see farther than a few yards, the desert stretched away on all sides, dark, mysterious, impenetrable. Just space, limitless space, and emptiness that was almost frightening. It was as if all the world had narrowed down to that one solitary trail, and we the only people in it.

CAMPING IN THE SAHARA

And when the light of the moon strengthened, throwing a silvery pathway across the rippling sand that appeared softly swelling like a peaceful sea, it only made the surrounding gloom more densely black, the feeling of remoteness and isolation more intense.

Like phantoms, with giant shadows that stalked beside, we moved in the midst of that great loneliness, herding together for very companionship, speaking, when we spoke at all, in voices that scarcely rose above a whisper.

Here in these mighty plains, under the vast canopy of heaven, the sense of man's insignificance rises up with crushing force, and only nature matters. Atoms we seemed, our little company a mere procession of feeble, plodding ants. While all around us lay in wait the desert's stupendous forces, that could, in a moment, dispel us, like atoms, into everlasting nothingness.

With the full light of the moon came a chilly wind, that whistled about our ears and drove the acrid smell of the camels back in our faces.

Now and again a tentative song rose from one and another of the men. But even they seemed to feel the strange spell of the night, and the songs would break abruptly to die away unfinished. And their voices were hushed as they talked together, their whistles faint as they urged the camels forward.

No other wanderers were abroad that night. And if there were nomads' camps hidden amongst the dunes—as there must have been—their watch-dogs did not scent the passing caravan.

All night long the wind blew intermittently in noisy gusts that came booming and shrieking over the desert to fade away in an eerie wailing that was like the crying of an animal in pain. But in the dark hour before the dawn it settled down to blow steadily, and the air grew bitterly cold. Numbed through, with hands and feet dead to all feeling, we gave up trying to guide the mules and left them to their own devices, which took them bumping and barging into the middle of the caravan. And there at least it was warmer, though somewhat smelly. But the camels didn't love us, and very quickly bumped and barged us back into the cold again.

At last the dawn came, a thin faint line on the horizon that widened and deepened slowly into a pinky flush. Then, as the light strengthened and the twinkling stars paled one by one and died, streaks and bars of crimson and gold shot across the sky and the rim of the sun rose up against a bank of fiery cloud.

In the cold early light even the men's brown faces looked grey; our own, I know, were blue.

With teeth chattering I rolled out of the saddle, and tramped for an hour before I felt there was anything more than lumps of lead in my riding-boots.

At five o'clock we halted for breakfast, and thawed out over a brushwood fire.

CAMPING IN THE SAHARA

There were nomads camping near, and furtive figures came slipping through the tall *drinn* bushes to peep and stare and slip away again.

And riding on, we met many others, camelherds mostly, in ones and twos, sauntering after their grazing charges or lying on the warm sand wrapped in dreamless meditation.

The herbage in this district is not suitable for sheep and we saw very few. But camels thrive on the dense coarse bushes, which sometimes were so closely set together that we had to force a passage through them, and that morning we passed among herds that were beyond counting.

Man is an inconsequent animal, and rarely satisfied. In the cold of the previous night we had longed passionately for the sun. By ten o'clock in the morning we were longing as passionately that a cloud might come to blot out the blinding rays that were scorching us through and through. But the sky was a bright hard blue with no cloud or hope of a cloud. So, as we had come far enough for one stage, we made camp there and then, in a tiny pocket in the dunes, and lazed away the rest of the day in peaceful idleness.

Four days later we reached Touggourt, pitching our last camp two miles outside of the town.

Here we had the unexpected pleasure of again meeting our friend the Caid of Hadjïera. Returning from business which had detained him in the north throughout the length of our trip, he reached Touggourt the same evening as ourselves and, hearing of our arrival, broke his journey to Hadjïera and rode into our camp at eleven o'clock that night, eager to hear all about the tour he had recommended but had never himself made.

PRINTED IN GREAT BRITAIN BY
RICHARD CLAY & SONS, LIMITED,
BUNGAY, SUFFOLK.

Lightning Source UK Ltd.
Milton Keynes UK
UKHW03f0851150318
319492UK00001B/50/P